Hope for Widows is a great companion for selves living alone.

Brenda F. Atkinson, MDiv, retired

God never wastes our grief. If we're willing to listen to His quiet, loving voice as He walks with us, we will learn to trust Him and lean on His grace, and we will begin to discover the treasures He has hidden along the path.

Erich Bridges, widower and retired journalist

Marilyn Nutter invites the reader into one of the most raw and intimate paths of her own journey—the days following the loss of her beloved husband. With the transparency of the broken, the strength of her character, the eloquence of her giftedness, and the foundation of her faith, she leads her readers down a road of understanding on how to regain equilibrium after a devastating loss and how one might minister to those who are still in that process.

Dan L. Burrell, EdD, pastor, LIFE Fellowship; associate professor and mentor, Liberty University

Marilyn Nutter is a gifted teacher and wise mentor who offers invaluable spiritual insight. This season of widowhood has served to make her testimony richer and deeper.

Kathy Dority, minister of connections, Taylors First Baptist Church

Transparent, honest, and sometimes raw, these short inspirational chapters provide hope-filled, God-centered messages to comfort the hurting and offer ways friends can come alongside widows to lighten their load.

Lori Hatcher, author of *Refresh Your Faith, Refresh Your Hope,* and *Refresh Your Prayers*

Marilyn Nutter . . . doesn't paint a false smile on grief but encourages the reader to look for the treasures that give meaning and help to times of mourning. This book is honest and practical.

M. Esther Lovejoy, author of *The Sweet Side of Suffering* and *Big Steps, Little Steps*

Hope for Widows will touch the hearts of all who read it. . . . You'll either want it because it applies directly to you, or you'll want to be able to use it to comfort those who are widows.

Edie Melson, author of *Soul Care While You're Grieving* and *Soul Care When You're Weary*

Finding hope in the midst of grief is a way through the sorrow toward the blessing of restoration. *Hope for Widows* guides you along the steps toward your unique pathway forward.

> Carolyn Moor, development director of the Modern Widows Club

For those who are grieving, Marilyn's words whisper: *You are not alone. Hope for Widows* invites readers to grieve the earthly loss of their loved ones, grieve the loss of dreams, and grieve future shared experiences. But, through this grief, Marilyn shows how widows can begin to live again.

> Erin Odom, author of *More Than Just Making It* and creator of thehumbledhomemaker.com

Hope for Widows offers meaningful encouragement to hurting hearts. Faith can be tricky when life doesn't turn out as we expect it to. This Scripture-based book will help clear away doubt, facilitate healthy processing, and bolster the faith of widows in and through their time of grieving.

> Gwen Smith, *Graceologie* podcast host, coach, author, and cofounder of Girlfriends in God

Marilyn takes us on a journey as she unfolds God's infinite grace found in the ebb and flow of her grief. From minute life circumstances to big events, Marilyn shows how God met her with grace and His all-sufficient love. Her words of wisdom penetrate the heart as a healing balm to those grieving and as insight for the ones who love them.

> Susan Wojcik, former counselor and women's ministry director of Life Fellowship

When a person writes their heart on a page, wise people pay attention and learn from their experiences. As a widow myself, I understand the pain and heartache Marilyn worked through toward her recovery. You too will come to treasure the solid, commonsense advice offered in this encouraging book.

> Brenda J. Wood, author of *The Pregnant Pause of Grief* and host of *Heartfelt* on Hopestreamradio.com

hope for widows

REFLECTIONS ON MOURNING, LIVING, AND CHANGE

Marilyn Nutter

Our Daily Bread
Publishing.

Published in association with Books & Such Literary Management, www.booksandsuch.com.

Requests for permission to quote from this book should be directed to: Permissions Department, Our Daily Bread Publishing, PO Box 3566, Grand Rapids, MI 49501, or contact us by email at permissionsdept@odb.org.

Scripture quotations, unless otherwise indicated, are taken from the Holy Bible, New International Version®, NIV®. Copyright © 1973, 1978, 1984, 2011 by Biblica, Inc.™ Used by permission of Zondervan. All rights reserved worldwide. www.zondervan.com.

Scripture quotations marked ESV are taken from the ESV® Bible (The Holy Bible, English Standard Version®), copyright © 2001 by Crossway, a publishing ministry of Good News Publishers. Used by permission. All rights reserved.

Scripture quotations marked MSG are taken from *The Message*, copyright © 1993, 2002, 2018 by Eugene H. Peterson. Used by permission of NavPress, represented by Tyndale House Publishers. All rights reserved.

Scripture quotations marked NASB are taken from the New American Standard Bible®, copyright © 1960, 1971, 1977, 1995, 2020 by The Lockman Foundation. Used by permission. All rights reserved. www.Lockman.org.

Scripture quotations marked NKJV are taken from the New King James Version®. Copyright © 1982 by Thomas Nelson. Used by permission. All rights reserved.

Scripture quotations marked NLT are taken from the Holy Bible, New Living Translation, copyright ©1996, 2004, 2015 by Tyndale House Foundation. Used by permission of Tyndale House Publishers, Inc., Carol Stream, Illinois 60188. All rights reserved.

Interior design by Michael J. Williams

Library of Congress Cataloging-in-Publication Data

Names: Nutter, Marilyn, 1946- author.
Title: Hope for widows : reflections on mourning, living, and change / Marilyn Nutter.
Description: Grand Rapids, MI : Our Daily Bread Publishing, [2024] | Summary: "Sixty-five interactive reflections guide widows to God's faithfulness in their upside-down lives, moving loss toward hope. Women will discover how, even in overwhelming grief, they can find treasures, purpose, and hope in a new journey marked by changes and challenges"-- Provided by publisher.
Identifiers: LCCN 2023029089 (print) | LCCN 2023029090 (ebook) | ISBN 9781640702844 (paperback) | ISBN 9781640702868 (epub)
Subjects: LCSH: Widows--Religious life. | Widowhood--Religious aspects--Christianity. | BISAC: RELIGION / Christian Living / Death, Grief, Bereavement | RELIGION / Christian Living / Family & Relationships
Classification: LCC BV4528 .N88 2024 (print) | LCC BV4528 (ebook) | DDC 248.8/66--dc23/eng/20230712
LC record available at https://lccn.loc.gov/2023029089
LC ebook record available at https://lccn.loc.gov/2023029090

Printed in the United States of America
24 25 26 27 28 29 30 31 / 8 7 6 5 4 3 2 1

To Randy Nutter, my biggest cheerleader, who
filled my heart with love and life.

To my widowed friends, who move forward and
lean into life with courage and grace.

To my Savior Jesus, for His incomparable life-giving grace each day.

And with thanks to my family and friends
for their encouragement and love.

CONTENTS

"You are a griever. Nothing will change the loss that has interrupted your life and made you a griever, so the question is not, 'What will I do about my grief?' Grief is not a problem to be solved. It is an opportunity to be seized. Neither is grief a destination. Grief is a process. Therefore the real question is, 'What will I do *with* my grief?'"

—Harold Ivan Smith, *ABCs of Healthy Grieving*

INTRODUCTION
Don't Miss the Treasures

Bless the Lord, O my soul, and forget not all his benefits.

PSALM 103:2 ESV

My husband and I wanted to do something different to celebrate our forty-second wedding anniversary. I love warm weather, so cool temperatures and minimal sunshine would be a stretch for me. But Alaska was on my husband's wish list, so I suggested we go. Our cruise turned out to be one of the best trips I've ever taken. And I'm thankful my husband and I experienced it together.

Each day a naturalist spoke passionately about sightings to anticipate as we cruised and when we docked. "Don't miss the treasures by comparing the cities you've come from with the land you'll see," he suggested.

Little did I know those words would be relevant in the months and years that followed.

He reminded us to breathe deeply of the purest air on the planet, to bask in some of the most magnificent scenery on earth, and to be awestruck at the gargantuan blue glaciers. We did. And we were.

And, while some of us were awestruck with God's creation and mesmerized by its beauty, others on board were holed up in casinos or sleeping on deck. They missed out.

Whether we were at sea or on land, each day brought fresh surprises. We savored the scenery and observed the beauty of God's creation we had previously seen only in movies or read about in books. Some of that scenery is captured in framed photos on walls in my home—treasured memories.

God knew the lecturer's words were a prelude to what would soon be my new status as "widow." Four months later, two days before Christmas, and two thousand miles from home, I heard the physician's words: "Your husband didn't make it. We did all we could."

Later, as I walked a single path on a new journey, I remembered the naturalist's thought: "Don't compare where you were with where you are."

Where we are as widows is not where we were. We look at life through new lenses as we try to adjust and accommodate. Communication changes. We speak of "I" not "we," "mine" not "ours." The contents of our refrigerator look different. Our friendships and social calendar shift. We circle "W" on information forms and file taxes as a single. Our checks and mail bear only our name. We have no one to share decisions—from handling finances to choosing paint colors, planting shrubs, and selecting presents for the grandchildren. We're sad and sometimes engage in self-pity. We're lonely. We agonize in prayer. To survive and grow, we need to learn and recalibrate.

Unlike my grandmother, who wore black after her husband died, today's widow has no way to show the world she mourns. How can people not realize? Yet at the same time, we wouldn't want our widowhood to define us. Yes, we're living a different life; but *widow* is only one of our labels, not our identity. We need to check and recheck our thoughts, remembering not to compare where we are with where we were. But on some days, it's difficult.

Cardiologists and counselors alike attest to the ill effects of stuffing our grief. Yet the timetable for a widow's grief journey is as unique as we are—our circumstances, ages, and personalities vary. God wired us to cry in sorrow, and we need to do so. We need to take time to mourn our loss by acknowledging life is different and working through it. Along the way, as time passes, we change.

On my grief and mourning journey, I began to see treasures through my tears. Over time, my experiences, new friends, and new skills increased my confidence, and I grew in my new reality. God met me and provided for me in unusual ways. Each lesson was a "treasure" to hold, examine, and then store for future use when I needed reminders of God's faithfulness in new challenges or when I became discouraged and lonely. They enabled me to reach out to other widows whose grief was fresh.

I write to share with you, a woman like me, living in a new season. As we journey together, you'll have the opportunity to record your treasures in your journal and, as you remember and reflect, jot down pieces of your story. As new discoveries continue, reread your entries and see how you're growing and changing. I know you'll weep, but you'll also smile. You'll look back but also ahead and hold on to the hope of our faith.

The vignettes in *Hope for Widows* are the outcome of some of my journal reflections.

As you reflect on your own story, ponder the words I heard on the cruise: "Don't miss the treasures." You have to look in order to see. As our Alaska guide so wisely said, we don't want to miss the treasures each day holds.

1

Life Flight and on the Road

For he will order his angels to protect you wherever you go.

PSALM 91:11 NLT

Our Christmas visit with family in Idaho began earlier than usual. We had expectations for a sweet time with loved ones we hadn't seen since summer. Our son-in-law, Paul, pastored a church in Lewiston, and the new building was scheduled for dedication a week before Christmas. Our grandchildren were also participating in a school Christmas program, and my grandson was celebrating a birthday, so we made travel arrangements to include the special events.

The dedication was full of excitement and gratitude for a journey that included years of preparation. My husband, Randy, took one photo after another that night. The following Sunday as we entered the new building for worship, I told him, "You've taken hundreds of photos. Let's get our picture to mark this occasion for us too." We'd visited Lewiston for twelve years, watched the church grow, and made friends there. This was a special moment I wanted framed.

We motioned to a friend who gladly took our picture in front of one of the beautifully lit Christmas trees in the gathering space. I never dreamed it would be the last picture we'd have together.

A few days later, Randy went to the church with Heather to help with sound for the children's choir rehearsal for Christmas Eve. When they got back, Randy was having chest pains. We rushed to the ER. The diagnosis was a major heart attack that required stents. The small hospital was not equipped to do the procedure, and he was life-flighted to Spokane, Washington. Heather and our youngest daughter, Kate, who had arrived the day before, led in one car, and I rode with my son-in-law in another. We stayed connected with surgeons in Spokane by cell phone.

During the drive, Dee, a dear friend, texted, "Hope you are having a wonderful time with your family." I responded with the news of Randy's heart attack and our travel to Spokane. She relayed it to others and news spread on Facebook. Hundreds were praying.

The two-hour trip on dark, snowy roads seemed like ten. We arrived at the hospital and went to the room number given us. The room was empty.

"He's still down in the cardiac lab," a nurse told us.

Another nurse directed us to the waiting room. We waited and wondered . . . and prayed. I prayed for my husband's protection. Months later I discovered how that prayer was answered.

Treasured Reflections: Photos are more than images frozen in time. They can evoke memories, tears, and smiles. I treasure that last photo of my husband and me. What about you? Do you have a photo that reminds you of a special time or conversation, or captures a "last" cherished moment? Scroll through the photos on your phone. Do any especially speak to you?

Treasured Thoughts: What comes to mind when you think about your last day(s) with your husband? Did friends visit or pray with you? Did you share a special conversation or activity? Did you spend time alone or with friends or family? Perhaps you worked together on a home project or enjoyed a favorite TV program. Journal your thoughts about your "lasts." Although they're bound to bring tears, focus on the treasures of time, love, and gratitude as you remember and write.

"Memories hurt, memories
help, memories heal."

Kenneth C. Haugk, *Rebuilding and Remembering*

2

The Waiting Room

To everything there is a season, a time for every purpose
under heaven: a time to be born, and a time to die.

ECCLESIASTES 3:1–2 NKJV

Even if the moments following your husband's passing are a blur,
most widows remember that day vividly. I do. Eleven years later,
I still see it clearly.

We entered an empty waiting room. Heather fell to her knees and
called out loudly in prayer. Paul communicated via cell phone with
family and our pastor—and paced. Kate stood and texted updates
to her sister Susan in Pennsylvania. I sat, thought, and prayed. Texts
came in reassuring us of prayer.

A chaplain entered the waiting room, introduced himself, and interrupted our intimate family time, making conversation when we didn't
want or need it. Perhaps it was his way of distracting us from our serious situation. A Spanish proverb, attributed to Jorge Luis Borges, says
"Don't talk unless you can improve the silence." The chaplain's words
and intrusion into our family time did not help alleviate our stress. He
eventually left.

A physician came in, sat next to me, and said my husband was having a "rocky time." The left anterior descending artery, commonly
known as the widow-maker artery, was significantly blocked. I told
him we were praying for both the medical team and my husband. He
left, returning about thirty minutes later with more ominous news.
They had to do CPR, and my husband was resting. "We're letting the
heart rest," he said.

I knew there was more he wasn't saying, but I couldn't bear to ask the question, "You're telling me he may not make it, aren't you?" I was afraid of the answer.

Two men from Paul's church, who just "happened" to be Christmas shopping in Spokane, hurried to the hospital when they received news of my husband's heart attack. Their presence was God-planned, as we would find out in the next hour. They quietly sat in the waiting room, heeding the wisdom of Ecclesiastes 3:7: There is a "time to be silent and a time to speak." To this day, I see their faces and am thankful for their sensitivity.

Thirty minutes later, three men in scrubs approached the waiting room. We stood and heard the words no one wants to hear: "I'm sorry. We did all we could. The blockage was too great."

Numb and shocked, we asked a few questions, and they left.

Later, as I saw my husband's body for the last time, I touched his beautiful thick gray hair and kissed him goodbye—for now. I'd waited in the waiting room, now I wait for our heavenly reunion.

Randy's heart was whole and at rest. Mine was broken.

Treasured Reflections: Did you have a waiting experience? Waiting for medical test results or for family to arrive at the hospital or home? What does your waiting look like now? How does the anticipated treasure of a heavenly reunion bring you comfort and hope in grief? "I wait for the LORD, my whole being waits, and in his word I put my hope" (Psalm 130:5).

Treasured Thoughts: Journal your thoughts about reunions and hope. What Bible promises comfort you?

"No one ever told me that grief felt so like fear."

C. S. Lewis, *A Grief Observed*

3

Silence and Sacrifice

. . . a time to be silent and a time to speak.

ECCLESIASTES 3:7

Was your body numb following the news of your husband's passing? Mine was. Our family stared at each other incredulously. How could we start a day together on such a happy note and have it end this way? For personal safety, medical personnel advised us not to drive the two hours to Lewiston that night. Our friends Don and Gary (who had been shopping in Spokane and sat with us in the hospital) volunteered to drive us back. Gary drove one of our cars and Don drove the other. They returned to Spokane the next day to get their car. Inconvenienced by snow, and a day before Christmas, they sacrificed with their gift of time.

Paul rode home with Gary. Kate, Heather, and I rode together in the back seat of the other car as Don drove. Stunned and in shock, we held hands, not speaking. At one point, Don looked in the rearview mirror and said, "I enjoyed all the times Randy and I went fishing together." Those were the only words he spoke. He had lost a son a few years before. Now I wonder if he was remembering his own painful loss as he viewed ours. At the least, he knew not to distract us with the attempted salve of meaningless talk. The remainder of the two-hour drive was silent.

We were profoundly thankful these dear men had gone to Spokane that day to shop. Their plans were disrupted, but God's plans for our provision were fulfilled.

Treasured Reflections: In the hours surrounding your husband's passing, who can you remember with gratitude? How do you see God's provision?

Treasured Thoughts: Have you ever written about that day? Would it be a step toward healing to remember how people came alongside you? What responses and comforting words come to mind?

"The friend who can be silent with us
in a moment of despair or confusion,
who can stay with us in an hour of grief
and bereavement, who can tolerate
not knowing . . . not healing, not
curing . . . that is a friend who cares."

Henri J. M. Nouwen, *Out of Solitude*

4

I Still Want to Sing . . . for Papa

Worthy are you, our Lord and God, to receive glory
and honor and power, for you created all things, and
by your will they existed and were created.

REVELATION 4:11 ESV

Widows dread the firsts: the first Valentine's Day, anniversary, birthday, and Christmas without a spouse. There's nothing magical about getting through each of the firsts. We endure them and move on to the seconds and the thirds. We may feel less pain, but the empty space in each special occasion remains.

We experienced our "first" Christmas the day after my husband passed. We had hardly slept in twenty-four hours. It was Christmas Eve. The phone calls and texts made and received seemed never ending. We looked at each other in disbelief as we tried to process Randy's unexpected death and to plan for the next few days: changing flights, contacting funeral homes, arranging for a memorial service back in Charlotte. It felt like a bad dream. My husband died far from home. Was that a problem? We had my grandchildren, ages five and seven, to think about. Our hearts were broken. Our minds were broken too—we could barely think straight. Making funeral arrangements is always difficult, but on Christmas?

Heather was supposed to lead the children's choir that night and Paul was supposed to preach. Paul arranged to go to the church and announce Randy's passing, and a staff member would preach in his place. Heather found a substitute. It was midafternoon when my granddaughter Elliott announced, "I still want to go and sing for Papa [her name for Randy]."

How do you tell a seven-year-old no at such a time? Perhaps it was her way to handle grief.

"Okay," Heather said, "but after you sing, we'll go home."

Heather drove Elliott to church an hour before the service and returned home. When she stepped in the door, Quinn announced he wanted to go too. The church was five minutes from their home, so Heather made another trip. Then Kate, Heather, and I drove back ten minutes before the service started. We stood in the back in our sweats. People passed us as they looked for seats, but no one recognized us. I didn't even recognize myself.

We watched as Quinn, dressed as a shepherd, ran down the aisle and stood beside the manger to gaze at the infant Jesus. The choir took their place on stage. With closed eyes, Elliott raised her arms to heaven as she sang. At that moment, one of Heather's friends took a picture of the children and sent it to Heather. Her thoughtful gesture at a time when we couldn't think straight was greatly appreciated. Sometimes simple gestures and gifts leave lasting impressions. I have the framed photo on my bookshelf.

God gave Elliott a song as she worshiped and sang for her Papa. In our pain, when we couldn't sing, we quietly embraced God's love and grace and listened. He gave us treasures from two children whose eyes were on Jesus while ours were full of tears.

Your thinking may remain cloudy and the tears may continue well after the initial shock. Perhaps you're wondering about the grief responses of the people in your family and how different they are from yours. It's good to keep in mind that just as our relationships and personalities are different, our grief expressions are also individual and personal. One grandchild may weep openly, while another retreats to be alone and a third shoots baskets in the driveway. Grief is personal.

Treasured Reflections: What treasures of love and grace have you seen in your grief journey? Did someone speak a sweet word about a memory or lighten your load on the day you made funeral plans? Did someone sit with you, bring a meal, or perform a simple but needed task?

Treasured Thoughts: Journal about the simple, yet meaningful responses from others to your loss.

"God gave us memory so that we might have roses in December."

James M. Barrie interview, "Thirty-Four Diamond Medals"

5

Only His Suitcase

I will be your God throughout your lifetime—until
your hair is white with age. I made you, and I will
care for you. I will carry you along and save you.

ISAIAH 46:4 NLT

Friends brought Christmas dinner for us that evening. We moved
the food around on our plates and finished in about ten minutes.
We had no appetite. Unknown to me, my son-in-law Paul graciously
packed my husband's suitcase. Once again, we drove to Spokane. This
was our third trip that week. We'd also driven there a few days earlier
to pick up Kate who'd flown in from Charlotte. Now we planned to
spend the night there and fly home early the next morning. Kate and
I were on one flight; Heather, Paul, and the grandchildren were on
another. How we found four seats on the same flight on December
26, and Kate and I together on another flight on the same date, was
miraculous.

At the hotel, Paul took the children down to the pool. When they
returned, the kids thought it was the best treat ever to sit on a bed and
eat microwave mac and cheese. Elli wore the pioneer American Girl
nightgown she'd received for Christmas. I still see her sweet face as she
sat cross-legged on the bed. It was a bright spot during a dark time.
Heather, Kate, and I chuckled at the sight. God gave us that little treasure during what seemed like a nightmare.

We took a shuttle to the airport at 5 a.m. the next morning, and
Kate and I checked in to get our boarding passes. The clerk checked
our luggage and said there would be a charge for the extra bag.

"Okay," I nodded, and opened my wallet to get my credit card.

Kate is normally a quiet person, so she surprised me when, in raw grief, she said to the clerk, "Can I tell you why we have that extra suitcase? My father died three days ago while we were out here, so we're going home with only his suitcase."

The clerk looked at us without a word, tagged the suitcase, and gave us our passes. I imagined she could read the grief in our faces. The idea of coming to Idaho with Randy and returning only with his suitcase was startling. He had carried me all our married life. I wondered who would carry me in the days and months ahead.

Treasured Reflections: What image speaks to you most about being alone with no mate to carry you? Can you rest in God's promises that He never leaves you, will comfort you, and gives you wisdom?

Treasured Thoughts: Journal your thoughts about a Scripture verse or passage that helps carry you through your sorrow. Here is one possibility: "He is before all things, and in him all things hold together" (Colossians 1:17).

"Sometimes we want greater clarity
when what we need is deeper trust."

Ann Voskamp on Facebook, January 30, 2020

6

First Contacts
and Unspoken Words

Bear one another's burdens, and so fulfill the law of Christ.

GALATIANS 6:2 ESV

When you met friends and family for the first time following your husband's death, you most likely wept and received hugs. Maybe you retold parts of the story surrounding his last days. My dear neighbors Linda and Don met us at the airport and were my first contact with friends in Charlotte. Like everyone else, they were stunned. They hugged us and shed tears. On the drive home, Linda turned and said something I will never forget, "You can tell me as little or as much as you want." What a generous statement.

I was in a fog. I don't remember if I told her anything.

Once home, I opened the garage door, and my perceptive friend went ahead of me. She turned on lights and her husband brought in coolers of food. "Do you and Kate want to walk around the house?" she asked.

I still don't know why, but I did, and went upstairs. The quiet was loud, and the weight was heavy. I felt a heaviness in my stomach that would become a familiar companion in coming months, as would a quiet house. We turned up the heat. Don confirmed the time Heather and her family would arrive and insisted he pick them up.

"Remind me who I'm looking for," he said. I showed him photos on my wall, pointing out Heather's family. Then he held up a sign he'd made with their last name and reassured me they would connect.

Linda waited at home with Kate and me. We exchanged few words. Her silent presence was a comfort. She was helping to carry and hold us together.

The kids arrived, and the new normal of being at Nonni's house without Papa began. No more hearing Randy's booming laughter and never again hearing my grandchildren say, "Papa," or my kids calling out, "Dad."

I'm overwhelmed as I reflect on my friends' sensitivity and respect. At each turn, their practical help, the meals they provided, and their loving presence were grace moments.

Grace meets me too when I no longer hear Randy's voice or the kids calling out his name.

Treasured Reflections: As you reflect, what treasures are you thankful for: sensitive friends, practical help, a grace moment?

Treasured Thoughts: Journal about the comfort and care you received from others in the early days of your grief.

"Food is symbolic of love when words are inadequate."

Alan D. Wolfelt

7

Ornaments and a Mess

Behold, I am the LORD, the God of all
flesh. Is anything too hard for me?

JEREMIAH 32:27 ESV

While we were waiting for my daughter Susan to arrive, Paul encouraged Kate, Heather, and me to get out of the house for a change of place. I had no energy to do it, but Heather needed some toiletries, so we drove to Target.

We walked from the parking lot to the entrance at a snail's pace. My legs felt heavy, like concrete. Entering the crowded store brought my first wave of reality: everyone's life seemed to continue, while mine had stopped. Years later, I came across a quote by freelance writer Nicole Gabert validating my thought: "I've learned that no matter how badly your heart is broken, the world doesn't stop for your grief." Does that express your thoughts and observations?

A post-Christmas sale was in progress, and I questioned how anyone could think of anything so trivial. But I too had *once* enjoyed after-Christmas bargains. The Christmas department was crowded and a mess. Carts were loaded. Seriously? Was it *that* important to save $2.99 on wrapping paper? My husband was dead!

We passed a bargain bin with boxes of ornaments; some had been opened and were missing one or two out of eight. Others were cracked, and a few shattered. A few people had tossed in other items they'd decided not to buy. Heather stopped. "Look at this," she said. "This is a picture of our life today. Broken and a mess."

I agreed. I looked at the boxes of ornaments minus one or two.

We were missing one. And it hurt so badly. In time, I knew the

31

Lord would mend my heart and fill the empty space, but one ornament would always be missing.

Treasured Reflections: Shattered, broken, absent. Be real about your life, but acknowledge the treasure of God's promises and healing process that occurs with time. Did you or a widowed friend experience your loss on or near a holiday? The freshness of grief around a holiday is painful; and years later, loss is still present. Grief knows no calendar. Sometimes, in our brokenness, healing moments come for us as we reach out to others.

Treasured Thoughts: Journal your thoughts about holidays, special events, and an empty spot. Is there a tradition you especially want to continue or discontinue? Voice your desire to your family. They won't know unless you tell them.

8

Family Reunion

Love bears all things, believes all things,
hopes all things, endures all things.

1 CORINTHIANS 13:7 ESV

My daughter Susan, her husband, Jon, and their children had spent Christmas with Jon's family in Pennsylvania. They drove to Charlotte on December 27. When I opened the front door and saw their faces, the scene played all over again: shock and the reality of loss, tears, and hugs. As extended family arrived, the scene rewound and replayed.

My sons-in-law are great friends. When they greet each other in typical guy fashion, it's a hug, smiles, pat on the back, and yelling each other's name. This time it was different. In my foyer, Paul and Jon tearfully embraced. Not a word was spoken, but their actions said much. They loved each other, loved their father-in-law, and shared their deep loss.

Paul and Jon took over. They screened calls and prepared the music and remarks for the memorial service; and Jon organized the photos for the service. They cleaned the kitchen and put the extra food people had dropped off in my freezer. I did nothing. When I relayed this to my brother, his comment was, "They did their job—taking care of you."

In those moments of brief clarity, I was reminded of how privileged I am to have such a family.

Treasured Reflections: We cry because we loved. Family, friends, and tears are gifts to be treasured.

Treasured Thoughts: Journal your moments of gratitude.

9

Untimely Plans:
A Memorial Service

Her husband has full confidence in her.

PROVERBS 31:11

My church family was amazing. My friend Susan coordinated a meal sign-up for our family of eleven who would be staying at my house. When one friend received the email, she went to check her calendar. When she returned to sign up, all spaces were already filled. When you consider the meal plan called for three meals a day for two weeks and then one meal a day for two more weeks, the only way to view it is extravagant love in action. I was beginning to see how my friends would carry me in my fresh grief.

My pastors came to the house to plan the service. Our church met in a school that was closed for the Christmas break, so they worked hard to find another location. As we discussed the service in our new location, we knew we had one hour; a wedding was scheduled that day. What would we sing? Who would play instruments? Which family members would speak? Would we show pictures? How would we accommodate out-of-town family and friends? There was a plethora of decisions to make.

My four grandchildren wanted to sing. At our last Thanksgiving at Susan's, we went around the table sharing what we were thankful for. Randy was thankful all his grandchildren knew Jesus. My five-, six-, and seven-year-olds wanted to sing "Jesus Loves Me." How fitting. We all needed that truth imbedded in our minds as we processed our grief.

Plans were finalized. Our pastor would speak, Paul would give the eulogy, and Jon and Susan would sing "Amazing Grace" to conclude the service. We asked a lifelong friend (now in heaven) to speak as a colleague and a friend. My daughters planned words of tribute to their dad.

What about me? Could I do it? The pastor wisely suggested we list "Randy's Girls" in the program as speakers. If I couldn't speak, no one would be the wiser. I prepared my words. I knew this might be the last time I could publicly talk about my husband; but still, I wondered if I could go through with it. I had not walked this way before.

On the morning of the service, I picked up my Bible and turned to the reading for the day—Proverbs 31. *How ironic*, I thought, *the virtuous woman, a wife. I'm no longer a wife but a widow.* It seemed like a cruel joke until I read, "Her husband has full confidence in her. . . . She brings him good, not harm, all the days of her life" (Proverbs 31:11–12). Randy was my biggest cheerleader, always encouraging me out of my comfort zone. Even in death, he cheered me on. I could still "bring him good."

Widows approach their husband's memorials in different ways. Some have others read their tributes. I chose to speak as my last way to publicly honor Randy. I treasure that to this day.

Treasured Reflections: What are five things to celebrate about your husband's life?

Treasured Thoughts: Journal about the expressions of help and kindness you've received. Offer a prayer of thanks for each one.

"But there is a discomfort that surrounds grief. It makes even the most well-intentioned people unsure of what to say. And so many of the freshly bereaved end up feeling even more alone."

Meghan O'Rourke, "Meghan O'Rourke on *The Long Goodbye*"

10

His Work Isn't Finished

He commanded our ancestors to teach them to their children, so
the next generation might know them—even the children not
yet born—and they in turn will teach their own children.
So each generation should set its hope anew on God, not
forgetting his glorious miracles and obeying his commands.

PSALM 78:5–7 NLT

Thinking back to the funeral or memorial service, were you numb or running on adrenaline? As we stood in line to walk into the sanctuary for the memorial service, my stomach was in knots. The girls turned to me like deer caught in headlights. My brother escorted me. He told the girls to take a deep breath. I told them, "Your ancestors crossed the ocean in the early 1900s. You can do this." To this day, I have no idea where that thought came from. It was true. My immigrant grandparents and father courageously left their country to come to America. God gave us the courage and strength we needed to take part in the service.

As we left the sanctuary after the service and headed upstairs for the reception, I stopped to talk with the host pastor. I thanked him for the use of his church and how appreciative our family was of the staff's kindness during this holiday season. He expressed his sympathy and told me he would pray for our family.

"It's hard for me to process," I told him. "A friend told me my husband's work was done, and it was his time. He was young and in the middle of teaching . . ." I'm not sure what else I said. Perhaps I rambled. I don't remember.

"Let me tell you," he said, "your husband's work is not done."

I remember looking surprised at his comment. He went on.

"I listened to the tributes from your children and grandchildren. Your husband left a beautiful legacy of faith. His work is not finished. It lives on."

Those words were a comfort, and still are, as I see my children, their mates, and grandchildren live out their faith. When I read about my husband's former students impacting the business world and raising beautiful families, I see truth in the pastor's words. To this day, they post remembrances of his influence in their lives on social media.

Legacy. I take joy because my husband lived to make a difference and that difference lives in others.

Treasured Reflections: Does the pastor's perspective change your thinking about when a person's work is finished? What consolation and joy do you receive from your husband's legacy?

Treasured Thoughts: Journal your thoughts about the legacy left by your husband's life and by your influence as a couple. Do you see a child or grandchildren pursuing your husband's academic interests or a hobby he loved? Do faith lessons he lived and shared continue to be part of your family's life? Did he mentor someone in the workplace, church, or neighborhood who still sings his praises or exhibits fruit from that relationship?

"Legacy. What is a legacy? It's planting
seeds in a garden you never get to see."

Alexander Hamilton in *Hamilton*
by Lin-Manuel Miranda

11

New Year's Eve

I will lead the blind by ways they have not known, along
unfamiliar paths I will guide them; I will turn the darkness
into light before them and make the rough places smooth.
These are the things I will do; I will not forsake them.

ISAIAH 42:16

My husband's memorial service took place on December 30. We were humbled by the presence of friends, family, and former colleagues and students who traveled great distances during the holidays to honor my husband and support us. Most left the following morning to head home. My children and grandchildren stayed with me for a few days following.

December 31 marked the end of a year that began with my husband and ended without him. Never in my wildest imagination did I think I would close 2011 as a widow. It was a new reality I wasn't ready for and still couldn't believe.

Friends brought meals for us, so our refrigerator was full, and food covered my kitchen counter. The grandchildren, who lived hundreds of miles from each other, loved the extra time together.

How do adults observe a holiday characterized by celebration and festivity but marred by pain and raw grief? Susan wisely directed us to a few videos online. We watched an innocuous episode of *I Love Lucy*. Most of that night was a blur—with two treasured exceptions.

I wanted our family to take communion together. I asked Paul, my pastor son-in-law, to direct it. He prepared the bread and wine, read from Scripture, and asked me to serve the elements. As I went around the circle of my precious children and their mates, looking at each one, I spoke "the body and blood of Christ" and offered the bread and cup. As we finished, I said, "This is what it's all about. This is our hope." We prayed and sat around until the Times Square ball dropped at midnight. *Happy New Year 2012* flashed on the screen. My stomach held that now-familiar weight. *Happy? He isn't here. How can this be a happy new year? He's not in my future.* What would 2012 look like for me? I was beginning a new year my husband would not see or share with me. Everything I would do from this point on would be without him.

The other exceptional moment was when Heather got up from her seat and announced, "I'm going to kiss my mom." And she did. The others and I hugged too. It was an indelible moment as I was reminded again of the loving family I had.

I was the odd one in the group without a mate. It was the beginning of being a single in a couple's world. Life was going to be radically different, and I would be traveling on an unknown path. Only later did I recall the words of Isaiah 42:16.

Treasured Reflections: On that New Year's Eve, my treasures were the love of my children and the hope of eternity. How have you tangibly experienced God's presence even in the darkness of your grief?

Treasured Thoughts: Journal about how you balance the here and now with thoughts of the eternal. How does God's promise in Isaiah 42:16 help as you move forward in a new, unfamiliar way?

"The story of my life did not
begin at my birth, and it will
not end at my death either."

Jerry Sittser, *A Grace Revealed*

Grief
An Individual Matter

How you grieve and what you choose to do and not do around the holidays is your unique choice. I chose to celebrate communion. The spiritual connection with my family and the confidence of eternal life through Jesus's death and resurrection were important to me.

A friend of mine often posts this birthday greeting on Facebook: "Have the kind of birthday you want, not what someone else wants for you." That's good advice for the holidays as well. Some widows remember with an empty chair or a candle. Some move holidays to a mountain cabin or beach setting. Others stay home and replicate what they always did—same time, place, and menu. Only you know what will contribute to your remembering and healing.

"But in all of the sadness, when you're feeling that your heart is empty, and lacking, you've got to remember that grief isn't the absence of love. Grief is the proof that love is still there."

Tessa Shaffer, *Heaven Has No Regrets*

12

Me? A Support Group?

Blessed are those who mourn, for they will be comforted.

MATTHEW 5:4

When I saw a brochure for a grief support group at the church that hosted my husband's memorial service, I wondered if I should check it out. I'd read that the emotions of grief peak four to six months following loss, and with my daughter's wedding coming up in July, I wanted to be as fully present as I could. I was hesitant but thought I'd give the support group a try.

Kate came with me. What I would have done without her is beyond me. She helped carry me at times when she could barely focus. We walked in and were greeted with a hug from the female leader. It seemed like a safe place. A few minutes later, others joined the group. The facilitator opened with prayer and a few words about the group. I could hear one woman crying even as the leader spoke.

Participants introduced themselves, briefly describing their loss. Some men and women cried as they spoke. Ours was the most recent loss. People were surprised we were there. I questioned if I had made the right decision. The woman we spotted crying when we walked in said she'd lost her husband four years ago. *Four years?* I thought. *Is this what it's like?* The hour and a half passed quickly.

Kate and I walked to the car. "What do you think?" I asked.

Instead of responding, my daughter asked, "What do *you* think?"

I laughed at my wise daughter's question.

I responded, "That woman lost her husband four years ago and was crying like it was last week. Is that the way I'm going to be? If I am, I'll just crawl in a hole."

"We won't let you be that way."

I did my assigned homework in the notebook given me and wondered if I should go back. My dear friend Susan suggested that when we look for a new church, we generally give it three visits. The first visit could have been an off day, so the second is an opportunity to see if it's different, and the third finalizes your decision. Why not do that before I decide? I agreed and went back.

I stayed for the entire series. I learned that the woman crying after four years was mourning the loss of the dog she'd gotten as company after her husband died. Another person in the group had multiple losses. There were reasons for their tears.

Kate came to some of the sessions, and the group found great joy in her upcoming wedding plans. Some topics were helpful and others weren't applicable to me, but I learned about listening and giving compassion to others whose situations were different or more difficult than mine.

One size does not fit all in grief or in groups. Support groups vary based on the facilitators, the participants, and a person's readiness. Grief is as unique and personal as an individual's fingerprints. I walked a few more steps in my grief journey. Now, years later, I facilitate a group.

Treasured Reflections: Have you considered a grief support group? You might look online to find one in your area. It may be valuable to you, but if you're not ready, wait. Be careful not to assume or jump to conclusions when observing someone else's grief.

Treasured Thoughts: Journal your response about the positives and negatives of your support group or books you've read on grief. What were your takeaways? Did you gain new insights? Be comfortable saying, "That's not for me."

"They [support groups] are wonderful places to discover that you are not going crazy! It takes a lot of courage, though, to attend one of the groups. . . . Grievers need to hear 'me too' from other grievers. Thus, groups are often ideal environments in which to stumble toward resolution with the loss as you share your experience with others who offer support and encouragement."

Harold Ivan Smith, *ABCs of Healthy Grieving*

13

Clearing My Throat

Like cold water to a weary soul is good news from a distant land.

PROVERBS 25:25

One of the hardest things about being a widow for me is having no one at home to talk to. Not just for help with decisions, but for conversation. About two weeks after my husband's passing, my friend Ellen phoned to see how I was doing. Ellen had been widowed over twenty-five years, so she'd personally known loss. Over the course of the conversation, she asked if I would be interested in having her phone me each morning at 7:30 "to have coffee" as she put it. She knew Randy had made morning coffee for the two of us to enjoy together, so I felt that void in my life as I started my day. I welcomed the idea.

Our calls continued for many years. Sometimes they lasted ten minutes, sometimes thirty. We shared updates on our families, our latest recipes, my writing, and her online teaching; and sometimes we lamented the world news.

I always cleared my throat before saying, "Hello." Ellen was the first person I spoke to each day. On occasion, hers was the only live voice I'd hear in a day. In today's media-driven culture, emails and texts provide communication—and I appreciate those—but nothing replaces interacting with a live voice.

Over six years ago now, Ellen passed from earth to heaven. It was all so sudden. I spoke with her as usual at 7:30 that morning and at 5:10 p.m. she was gone. I miss her "mourning" call.

Treasures in a phone call? Absolutely. She was a perceptive, caring friend who kept a commitment, shared life, and gave me an opportunity to clear my throat.

Treasured Reflections: Have you recently expressed thanks for a phone call or in-person conversation? Perhaps you could initiate a call. Today, instead of a text, card, or email, try phoning a friend.

Treasured Thoughts: Do you have a friend or family member you enjoy talking with and who helps meet your need for conversation? Journal about it. Perhaps one day you can be that friend to another widow.

14

Deleted

But he said to me, "My grace is sufficient for you,
for my power is made perfect in weakness."

2 CORINTHIANS 12:9

One of the last things a grieving widow feels like doing is the te-dium of making phone calls to businesses, standing in lines, and rummaging through paperwork. One friend told me that folders and papers covered her dining room table for six months. Add to that the confusing and often painful, jumbled mess of locating account num-bers and user IDs, pressing endless numbers on a touch phone, and recalling passwords. We wonder how we got to this place and when it will all end. Eight months later, I was still changing accounts to reflect my newly widowed status.

Another thing I puzzled over in the months after my husband's death was some of the insensitive comments I received. Most comments were well-meaning, but as a grieving widow, they hurt. Some people didn't know what to say and so said nothing. That's better than comments such as, "It is what it is." (Yes, someone told me that.) Another com-ment right up there was, "Marilyn, the Lord will be your husband." A woman told me that while preparing to take an anniversary trip with her husband. *Really?* There were others, and every widow can recite them. They are lessons for us in what not to say.

In the many phone/business conversations I had with people, I en-countered only two rude individuals soon after my husband died. One clerk didn't "get" how painful the process of changing an account from two names to one can be. "So you want to take his name off?" She repeated coldly.

"Yes," I said, with my voice trembling. "He's deceased."

"I'll need some information." I supplied what she needed, and it was all business. "Okay, that's it," she announced. "His name has been deleted. Is there anything else?"

Anything else? "Uh, no, that's it." We said goodbye, and it was done. I wanted to shake her! *Don't you realize what this means?* I shouted to myself. I hung up in disbelief. Other voices offered condolences. Total strangers were compassionate. This one, not so much.

With a simple touch to a keyboard, a name—my husband's name—was deleted. It's as if he never existed—at least for that business account. I needed grace to complete that call and cross out that task on my "to do" list. When I put away the file, I thought about that clerk. I knew she needed prayer to develop understanding for others, but at that moment it was hard for me to pray.

Treasured Reflections: In what overwhelming task have you felt God helping you through? Perhaps you're facing one now. God's presence and promises are treasures on our hardest days. When I told a friend about waiting in line at the DMV for several hours, she told me she would have gone with me had I asked. People don't know our needs. Don't be afraid to ask for help.

Treasured Thoughts: Journal about a time God gave you the grace to be gracious to someone. How do you show grace to seemingly insensitive people? Make a mental note that they may not understand or be sensitive to your grief because they've never experienced loss.

"What we've got here is
failure to communicate."

The Captain in *Cool Hand Luke*,
directed by Stuart Rosenberg

15

Secondary Losses

Teach us to number our days, that we
may gain a heart of wisdom.

PSALM 90:12

Are you tired? My widowed friends say they have trouble falling asleep. God did not give us a forty-eight-hour day when our husbands died. We have the same amount of time to do double the work. Now we do it all: taking out the trash, weeding gardens, making appointments with repairmen, buying tires, and changing cable companies. "I'm doing what I always did at home plus doing the chores my husband did. Every time I roll the trash to the curb, I am reminded I'm alone," one friend told me.

In my grief support group, one of the topics covered was secondary losses. The workbook lesson that week included a question asking us to list five. I listed the first five that came to mind. The first was my husband's kiss on my head and hands on my shoulders each morning as he joined me in our morning room. I sighed and thought, *Only five? Really?* I took out my journal and began my list. Over the next days and months, I enumerated 175. Yes, I stopped there.

I know, by definition, our primary loss is the departure of the person we loved. But aren't the physical things that person did also primary? I reviewed my list as I wrote: "No dad walking my daughter down the aisle, not hearing my grandchildren say 'Papa,' no one to talk with during my evening meal (whenever I have an appetite to cook), no one to talk over decisions, no vacation planning, no spontaneous evening out, no morning coffee together, no sharing moments with grandchildren. . . . They are all tangible, physical losses; primary to my existence, significant in my daily living."

Years ago, I cut out a cartoon from the newspaper. In it, Ziggy says, "How come our saddest sadness comes from what was once our most joyous joy?" Ziggy apparently knew about losses.

The most joyous joys were treasures, and in their absence is sadness. With time and healing we begin to see those moments move into treasured memories. When grace meets us, they are priceless gifts.

Treasured Reflections: Have you made a list of your secondary losses? How do gratitude and grace accompany those treasured memories?

Treasured Thoughts: Sometimes when we perform a task that was our husband's responsibility or forte, waves of grief rush over us. Suddenly after weeks of taking out the trash, we may break down in tears and don't understand why. At such times, we're grieving secondary losses. Sometimes these experiences become triggers. Making a list to identify secondary losses may be helpful. Journal about your losses and what they mean to you.

"The reality is that you will grieve forever. You will not 'get over' the loss of a loved one; you will learn to live with it. You will heal and you will rebuild yourself around the loss you have suffered. You will be whole again, but you will never be the same. Nor should you be the same nor would you want to."

Elisabeth Kübler-Ross & David
Kessler, *On Grief and Grieving*

16

Choices and Control: Today

Behold, I am doing a new thing.

ISAIAH 43:19 ESV

D o you sometimes feel your life is out of control? You may feel that way because you've lost your mate. Those feelings are compounded if he was the one who managed most of the household responsibilities and had things "under control." My husband was a whiz at making airline reservations. He managed our finances and major household matters like our heating and cooling system. He even paid the bills. Though I always took part in big decisions, he did the research. Now I, like you, do it all.

If you're in your first year of loss, you're also closing or changing accounts and looking for and filing paperwork. If you're doing things outside your skill set and comfort zone, you may feel overwhelmed by all the new information to process and not have enough energy and time to deal with it. Ironically, control is what we widows have! It's a paradox.

On other levels, we have choices every day. I joked with someone that one of my perks is I can choose to paint my kitchen purple if I want, no discussion necessary. It's my choice. I have control! (But I'd much rather have my husband here with me in my kitchen.)

One of my widowed friends says she can barely get out of bed in the morning. Another has chosen to immerse herself in activity to lessen her aloneness. One friend in our grief support group said she can't think straight and forgets what to do unless she writes it on her calendar. Another volunteers for a nonprofit organization. Nearly all say they have no desire to cook and don't eat balanced meals. Some choices are healthy, and some aren't. Just as indulging in a hot fudge sundae twice a week might not matter in a month, over a year, we'll see the unhealthy effects. Lack of sleep, poor diet, too much or too little activity, or little exercise will catch up with us.

In our grief and loss, our thinking may be cloudy and decision making difficult. We're suffering emotionally, physically, mentally, and relationally. But we can make at least one healthy choice today. Try one of these:

Just for today, I will greet the sunrise with thanksgiving.

Just for today, I will say a prayer, even a sentence prayer, to start my day.

Just for today, when I lay my head on my pillow, I will be thankful I got through the day.

Just for today, I will be thankful someone came into my life to help me with something I didn't understand or know how to do.

Just for today, even if I cry, I will choose joy.

Just for today, I will read a short devotion or Bible passage.

Just for today, I will set my alarm and wake up earlier than yesterday to savor a cup of tea or coffee before all the busyness of the day.

Just for today, I will call a friend rather than wait for my phone to ring.

Just for today, I will plan to start something new—a book, a hobby, exercise.

Just for today, I will choose to make a meal, rather than snack.

Treasured Reflections: What resonated with you in the above reading—cloudy thinking, overactivity, sleeplessness? What is one unhealthy choice you make?

Treasured Thoughts: Write a list of the healthy options. Today is a start. Which will you try?

Self-Care
Healthy Choices

- Manage sleep. Stimulation from phone and computer screens can make it harder to fall asleep. Everyone is different as to how much sleep they need. Aim to wake up physically rested.
- Make healthy food choices. Watch empty calories and too much sugar. Drink water and monitor caffeine. Eat a meal, not a snack.
- Try to be physically active. Walk in a mall so you are around people. Perhaps walking around your neighborhood or joining a gym appeals to you. There are phone apps to track your steps and miles. Find a friend to walk with. Set personal goals.
- Guard against overactivity and becoming overtired.
- Monitor the TV programs you watch. Avoid sad movies or programs with tension and violence.
- Don't use lots of activity to cover up your grief. It may backfire, and you'll be exhausted.
- Call a friend. Do something that interests you, and/or plan a short trip or day trip.
- Write plans on your calendar so you have something to look forward to.
- Give yourself applause for whatever you accomplished today—the laundry, supermarket shopping, a clean cupboard, a decision.
- Get a pedicure, manicure, haircut, or massage.
- If you need help managing your loss, speak to a counselor or join a support group.
- If you have new physical symptoms, see your doctor to address them.
- Allow yourself to grieve in the way that's right for you.

"I have discovered that busyness and exhaustion can sabotage healing."

Jerry Sittser, *A Grace Disguised*

17

Upside Down

Whom have I in heaven but you? And there is nothing on earth
that I desire besides you. My flesh and my heart may fail, but
God is the strength of my heart and my portion forever.

PSALM 73:25–26 ESV

My youngest daughter, Kate, single at that time, taught at a school
ten minutes from my house. It was good for both of us that
we didn't live alone the few weeks after my husband's passing, so she
moved in with me. One evening, standing in the kitchen trying to figure out if I wanted to eat, and if so, what to fix, I called to Kate. She
was seated on a couch a short distance from me, reading a magazine.

"Kate, do you want any supper?" No answer. "Kate, what would
you like to eat? Kate?" She looked up, and I asked again. At this point,
we were both content with cheese and crackers or a bowl of oatmeal, so
I knew meal preparation was a snack or microwave preparation at best.

"Uh . . . ," she answered tentatively, "nothing right now." She looked
back at her magazine and then turned it right-side up. She looked up at
me. "Grief brain. I didn't even know it was upside down. I guess I was
staring, not reading." It provided both of us with a weak laugh.

That describes grief: an upside-down life. From making decisions
to a change in lifestyle, everything in a widow's life is upside down.
Early on, we stare and can't think clearly. Seeing our "single" status
checked on a form proves our life has been turned upside down. Sign-
ing a birthday card with only our name gives more evidence. Talking
to a car mechanic resembles a foreign language. You answer the phone
at 10 a.m. and clear your throat, realizing you haven't spoken a word
to anyone since you woke up.

Life is upside down and not the way I envisioned it at this age. Is that how you feel?

Lewis Carroll's Alice said, "It would be so nice if something made sense for a change." Eventually, life begins to change shape and make sense. You grow familiar with the paperwork needed to file income taxes (or even do it yourself); the single signature is the new normal; you have a service record on your car and can even talk with reasonable intelligence and familiarity on maintenance. Life is taking a turn. But we know we'll never see things as they were, because they aren't the way they were. But instead of upside down, the magazine is beginning to turn. Upside down to sideways.

Gradually, as life changes, we see treasures. One day it will almost be right-side up, but it will never be the same as it was. The words will always be a tad off.

Treasured Reflections: Is your life upside down, or do you see it moving to a new angle? Each turn is a measure of growth. Who has come alongside you to help ? Has a friend given guidance through tax preparation or help with a major purchase or decision?

Treasured Thoughts: Journal your thoughts about the angles of your life. Where do you see changes?

18

A New Perspective

[He was] a man of sorrows and acquainted with grief.

ISAIAH 53:3 ESV

The observance of Lent was not part of my early church tradition. As I observed others' practices, I associated Lent with giving up something as a sacrifice. One of my cousins gave up watching TV. I was always impressed with his willpower as a child. One of my daughter's high school friends gave up chocolate and turned down my tempting offer of chocolate ice cream when she came to our house. The idea was to give up something that "cost you."

In recent years, Lent has played a larger part in some evangelical observances. It's not associated so much with a personal sacrifice but with "giving up something to get more of God." In other words, the focus is not on the "thing" given up but on craving more of Jesus. The "heart" of the practice is preparing your heart for Easter. With that in mind, I read a book of forty meditations following Jesus from the garden of Gethsemane to the resurrection, moving me along a forty-day journey to Easter.

When I read about Jesus's agony in the garden and His overwhelming grief, I wept.

As a woman who had been grief-stricken for only a few months, I was reminded again that Jesus knows grief and feels my pain. He relates to me and sorrows with me. When Scripture says, He was "tempted in every way, just as we are" (Hebrews 4:15), it refers to His experiences not only of hunger, sleep deprivation, and rejection but also of grief. For me, it was a comfort to know Jesus wept in grief over Jerusalem, as people refused to see who He was. He wept over

Lazarus's death and the sorrow it meant for Him and Lazarus's family. He wept over what He was about to face on the cross.

The shortest verse in the Bible, "Jesus wept" (John 11:35), speaks to me and offers comfort. Jesus experienced sorrow. He knew what it meant to grieve.

Why did I weep as I read? I wept over Jesus's pain but also because my Savior knows my hurts, the pain of my loss, and the comfort I need. He sympathizes and empathizes with me. He has never overlooked me.

As I continue to walk through my labyrinth of grief, I meet the Man of Sorrows personally. I exchange no words because He already knows. He accompanies me on the difficult paths, times I feel I can't take one more step, and the moments when I catch my breath. Yes, I have a Savior who loves me and died for me, but who also knows my loss and my grief. He wraps His arms around me every day. He cares and weeps with me.

Treasured Reflections: What aspect of Jesus do you need today? His comfort or compassion? Search the Scriptures and see what He tells you about who He is. Remember, all His promises are "yes." Sometimes widowed friends are the hands, feet, and heart of Jesus to each other. Are you led to be one of those to another widow—to do something tangible, to offer companionship, to weep with her, to listen, or to hold her tight?

Treasured Thoughts: Journal about who Jesus is to you. How has faith sustained you?

"We were promised sufferings. They were part of the program. We were even told, 'Blessed are they that mourn,' and I accept it. I've got nothing that I hadn't bargained for. Of course it is different when the thing happens to oneself, not to others, and in reality, not imagination."

C. S. Lewis, *A Grief Observed*

19

English Class Essays
and Other Discoveries

But he said to me, "My grace is sufficient for you, for
my power is made perfect in weakness." Therefore I
will boast all the more gladly about my weaknesses,
so that Christ's power may rest on me.

2 CORINTHIANS 12:9

One of the assignments in my high school English class was to write a compare-and-contrast composition. You probably recall the task too: the teacher assigned a topic and students were to show the similarities and differences between two related aspects of that topic. We might compare and contrast having a cat or dog for a pet or living in a year-round warm climate versus experiencing the change of seasons. As we think about it, life is full of compare-and-contrast experiences. In April, just a few months after my husband's passing, I lived through dramatic ones.

My youngest daughter, Kate, lives locally. On Thursday, my other two daughters flew into Charlotte for a long weekend. We had a plethora of events scheduled, but when my oldest daughter, Heather, arrived, her luggage did not arrive with her. Initial inconvenience evolved into thinking about plans B and C.

The contents of Heather's luggage were significant: her bridesmaid dress for her sister Kate's July wedding was in it, and she had scheduled a fitting for alterations the next morning. She also had her cake decorating supplies to decorate mini cupcakes for Kate's bridal shower that Saturday. Susan, my middle daughter, who went to meet Heather, kept me informed from the airport via texts as attempts to locate the luggage failed. Scanners weren't functioning, so the airlines couldn't pinpoint the location.

The airline representative agreed Heather needed toiletries and clothing and gave permission for purchases if her luggage didn't arrive on a midnight flight. She generously offered to have her buy another bridesmaid dress off the rack if she could find one, and the quick-thinking clerk said, "Oh, and you'll need to buy shoes in order to hem the dress."

There was something else in the suitcase: a photo album for me and clothing Heather wanted to wear as we completed the final memorial of my husband's December passing—a graveside service with the four of us. The clerk looked at Heather incredulously as Heather finished the list of reasons as to why she *really* needed the suitcase. The clerk's facial expression revealed she knew no one could make up such a story. We stayed up until midnight, hoping the suitcase was on the last flight in. It was not. The drama continued into the next morning when it finally arrived.

Later that day we went to the cemetery to see their dad's headstone and place flowers on his grave. As we stood back and read his name on the tombstone, it seemed surreal. I looked at the beautiful tulips and hydrangeas Susan had chosen, and then stared at Randy's headstone. *Those beautiful and fragrant flowers don't begin to compare with what you're seeing in heaven with its perfect beauty and a perfect Savior*, I thought.

Our weekend contained the segments of a perfect compare-and-contrast composition. Two sisters from opposite parts of the country flying from their homes to mine. The worry of lost luggage (material things), while relishing the safe arrival of my daughters and a priceless reunion with family. Pondering a life well-lived as we stood at my husband's headstone on Friday—someone gone much too soon but now in a perfect home with Jesus; and on Saturday, a sweet, life-affirming bridal shower for Kate, a celebration of her new adventure with a young man handpicked by God.

My compare-and-contrast experiences that weekend held countless treasures.

Treasured Reflections: Can you discover treasures in the compare-and-contrast moments of your grief journey?

Treasured Thoughts: Journal your compare-and-contrast experiences.

20

Resurrection

The angel said to the women, "Do not be afraid, for I know that you are looking for Jesus, who was crucified. He is not here; he has risen, just as he said. Come and see the place where he lay."

MATTHEW 28:5–6

On my first Easter alone, my future son-in-law's family invited me to spend Easter with them. It was a gracious invitation, but my grief was so fresh—less than four months old. I honestly didn't know how I would feel about being with people I didn't know well when I was still emotionally fragile. It was one of those "firsts," a holiday without my husband. I confess I waited until the night before to confirm I was coming.

Before heading to their home, Kate and I attended the Easter service at church. The service and sermon were perfect—exactly the tone that ministered to me. It was reverent but celebratory, not lively and over the top, but also not stoic as if we had no reason for joy. God had designed a perfect service for me. Some might say it's presumptuous to think that way, but our God is a personal God. Psalm 139 tells us that.

As I stood to sing, I thought about my husband singing in heaven. I thought about the hope we have because our Savior lives. Jesus has defeated death, and one day we will live with Him. But right now, He is a living Savior for us, every single day.

Treasured Reflections: Will reading the account of the resurrection be a comfort and a treasure for you today, not only for eternity but for now? Do you know another widow experiencing a first Easter? How can you encourage her?

Treasured Thoughts: Journal your thoughts about your first Easter, the joy of believers, and power of the empty tomb. Reflect on 1 Corinthians 2:9 (NLT): "No eye has seen, no ear has heard, and no mind has imagined what God has prepared for those who love him." How do those words bring you comfort and hope?

21

Comforters

They have proved a comfort to me.

COLOSSIANS 4:11

"So which comforter are you getting?" I asked my daughter Kate, as we looked around the bedding department at her bridal registry selections.

"Well, I thought this would match the paint colors, and I might be able to use the curtains I already have," Kate explained, as she pointed to the comforter and shams she and her fiancé had selected.

Finding the right comforter for a bed can be a time-consuming project. It wasn't just about the color and the pattern, but also the weight. As I unfolded the comforter, I ran my hands across it, admiring the pattern.

"It's perfect," I said.

Colors, patterns, weight, variety . . . comforters.

In his letter to the Colossians, Paul writes about two men, coworkers, who proved a comfort to him. The Old Testament character Job had three friends who were (supposedly) comforters. They asked tough questions and pointed their fingers at Job. Hardly a description of a comforter I'd want in my life.

Fortunately, I had many true comforters in the months following my beloved husband's passing. Friends supported me in a variety of ways, from lunch out to bringing dinner in. From praying for and with me to listening as I expressed what was on my mind and in my heart. They reminded me of God's promises while recognizing my pain and that the reality of my situation could not be taken away. They helped with home maintenance and surprised me with a birthday cake. Friends anticipated needs or asked how they could help. Phone calls, texts, and emails seemed to arrive at just the right time. A walk with neighbors around my community and stopping to sit on a bench by our lake was a respite. My devotional reading also seemed tailor-made for me and my life season—the words of comfort and God's love for me popped off the pages.

Every form of comfort was Godsent, but . . . those words of comfort and warm friendships did not change my loss or life situation, nor did they remove my grief. I still cried, but friends comforted me and helped lighten the weight of my loss. Each provided what I needed when I needed it and became part of the new pattern in my life.

No finger pointing; no platitudes. They were true and proven comforters. I thank God for each of these treasures.

Treasured Reflections: What comfort have you received from friends and elsewhere? Thank God for those treasures. Remember as well to draw on His strength and character. He is a weight-bearer and lifter of your soul. In John 14:16 He promised not to leave us comfortless. We can trust Him because He keeps His promises.

Treasured Thoughts: Sometimes it's hard to see simple comforts through tears, but think and journal thoughts about the varieties of comfort you have received from friends, devotions, books, a grief group, a sermon, music, etc. What has spoken to you most?

"They may not need me; but they might,
I'll let my head be just in sight;
A smile as small as mine might be
Precisely their necessity."

Emily Dickinson, "They may not need me"

22

A Crumpled Candy Wrapper

Let us hold fast the confession of our hope without
wavering, for he who promised is faithful.

HEBREWS 10:23 ESV

I found an old purse in my closet. I opened it and pulled out a package of tissues, two pens, and a crumpled candy wrapper. The wrapper looked like one of those that had a "promise" written in it, so I was curious to see what philosophical message awaited me. When I opened it, much to my amazement it was blank.

My mind immediately went to empty words and unfulfilled promises. "Let's get together soon," a friend tells you when you unexpectedly see her in a supermarket. But it doesn't happen. A repairman schedules an appointment for noon, but at 2:00 you're still waiting. "But she told me she would invite me to her birthday party," a six-year-old cries, finding out she was excluded. Like my candy wrapper, words and promises sometimes prove empty. We're left disillusioned and disappointed.

In grieving, I've been fortunate to have the support and prayers of friends and family. But, at the end of the day, my house is occupied by me alone. When I go out and return home, I close the door behind me and enter silence. The sinking feeling in my stomach is heavy. There's no one there to say hello, ask about my time with friends, give me news about a friend or family member, or let me know about an email I need to read. No one to ask me if I want to go to dinner or a movie later, to make travel plans with, or to offer an opinion or advice. . . . Do you miss that physical, relational, and emotional presence?

At the end of the day, it's only me and God. His Word and promises have not been empty. He is faithful. He never leaves me or forsakes me (Hebrews 13:5). His words are encouragement, truth, and treasures.

Treasured Reflections: Words matter. I fill spiral-bound index cards with Bible verses that encourage me. Perhaps that practice, or writing verses on sticky notes for your mirror, would be helpful to you. Remember to leave on lights when you leave the house. If you've been out with single friends, check to see if you all made it home safely.

Treasured Thoughts: Journal responses to Bible verses that are special to you.

"On every page of the Bible there are words of God that give us reason to hope. . . . In the promises of God, I find inspiration and new hope."

Charles L. Allen, *The Miracle of Hope*

Scriptures of Confidence and Comfort

You can look up Bible verses online at sites like BibleGateway (https://www.biblegateway.com) by searching for a word, phrase, or Bible reference. You can choose your preferred version from the list of more than fifty options. Here are some that speak to me.

Abraham was "fully assured that what God had promised, He was able also to perform." (Romans 4:21 NASB)

When I am afraid, I put my trust in you. (Psalm 56:3)

Trust in the LORD with all your heart and lean not on your own understanding; in all your ways submit to him, and he will make your paths straight. (Proverbs 3:5–6)

May the God of hope fill you with all joy and peace as you trust in him, so that you may overflow with hope by the power of the Holy Spirit. (Romans 15:13)

If any of you lacks wisdom, you should ask God, who gives generously to all without finding fault, and it will be given to you. (James 1:5)

So with you: Now is your time of grief, but I will see you again and you will rejoice, and no one will take away your joy. (John 16:22)

"For I know the plans I have for you," declares the LORD, "plans to prosper you and not to harm you, plans to give you hope and a future." (Jeremiah 29:11)

Great is our Lord, and abundant in power; his understanding is beyond measure. (Psalm 147:5 ESV)

"For my thoughts are not your thoughts, neither are your ways my ways," declares the LORD. "As the heavens are higher than the earth, so are my ways higher than your ways and my thoughts than your thoughts." (Isaiah 55:8–9)

For this God is our God for ever and ever, he will be our guide even to the end. (Psalm 48:14)

Because of the LORD's great love we are not consumed, for his compassions never fail. They are new every morning; great is your faithfulness. (Lamentations 3:22–23)

The one who calls you is faithful, and he will do it. (1 Thessalonians 5:24)

Ah, Sovereign LORD, you have made the heavens and the earth by your great power and outstretched arm. Nothing is too hard for you. (Jeremiah 32:17)

Visit www.marilynnutter.com and download
"Thirty-One Days of Prayer for Those Who Grieve."

23

Spools of Thread

There is a time for everything, and a season
for every activity under the heavens.

ECCLESIASTES 3:1

On some days, I feel as if I am in a labyrinth floundering to find my way through projects on a to-do list. I move, turn around, and make little progress. Does that resemble your day?

Last week, I had a burst of energy and decided to clean out drawers and declutter. I sorted through odds and ends and old receipts, picked up stray paperclips, and threw out pens that no longer had ink. I filed my greeting cards according to categories so I could easily find cards for a specific occasion, rather than sort through twenty just to find a get-well card.

I tackled the sewing drawer and untangled loose thread of one color wrapped around a spool of a different color. Some stray ends were in knots. Straight pins were scattered in the drawer. I found three bobbins; and since I no longer own a sewing machine, I tossed those in the trash. A thimble I never used, and spare buttons—still in small plastic bags that had accompanied clothing I no longer owned—added to the trash. Sound familiar to you? I sorted and looked at the array before me. It might have been clutter at first glance, but it held more.

I identified each color of thread with a garment I or a family member once wore. I found a button that matched a blue plaid dress I wore as a teacher many years ago. I spotted the thread I used when I smocked dresses and nightgowns for my daughters. There were spare buttons for the long-sleeved shirts my husband wore to work. I found my embroidery thread for projects now hanging on my wall. I laughed as I saw colors that were fashionable "then" but definitely not now! My spread of colors, spools of thread, sewing items no longer needed, and the fancy straight pins used to attach yards of tulle to the head table at my oldest daughter's wedding—all reminded me of the colors and seasons in my life.

My little girls, who once wore smocked dresses, are now young women with families of their own. And as a widow, I no longer have men's shirts hanging in my closet. As I lingered and reflected, tears filled my eyes. I saw God's faithfulness in each thread and the seasons of life they symbolized.

Treasured Reflections: Can you give thanks today for the "threads and colors" people and experiences have brought into your life seasons? How have they enriched your past and present?

Treasured Thoughts: What about today's colors? Are many of your days gray, or do you see bursts of color emerging in new skills or opportunities? Have you befriended a new widow in her grief and added color to her life? Look around. Someone may be praying for a friend, and you may be her answer. Or perhaps one has entered your life to link arms with you in comfort and friendship.

"Father, help me to see the dark threads,
too, as part of Your design,
And so learn to trust You in all things."

Elizabeth Sherrill, *Journey into Rest*

24

Perfect Timing

For there is a time and a way for everything,
although man's trouble lies heavy on him.

ECCLESIASTES 8:6 ESV

Two weeks before Kate's wedding, we went to the mall and ran into Ann. We knew each other casually when we lived in Virginia nearly thirty years earlier. We attended the same church, and our daughters were in grade school together. Life happened. Her daughter died from post-surgical complications in 1999. Ann, her husband, and their son moved to Charlotte, and seven years later, her husband lost his battle with cancer. I told her about Randy's passing. We talked for a short time and promised to connect on Facebook after Kate's wedding. We did.

Ann attended another church, but I invited her to worship with me one Sunday. She accepted, liked it, and settled in. Each Sunday we went to lunch together. We had so much to catch up on that we often stayed until the menu and prices changed to reflect dinner. With Kate's move to another state, our Sunday lunches eased the pain of eating Sunday lunch alone and going back to an empty house after church.

Ann was further along in her mourning journey than I was. In many ways, she was my mentor. She encouraged me, shared my loss, recommended books to read, affirmed my feelings as normal, and told me to take my time.

Her new normal showed me there was hope and purpose. We went to a retreat, concerts, and met for dinner and shopping. She was the only widow I knew, and she filled a void in my life. More than that, she was a gift at the time I needed a friend who understood the changes widowhood brings.

Running into Ann was a treasure, as were the next two years that followed. I am eternally thankful for my casual friend from Virginia who years later became a mentor, special friend, and God's perfect provision at the right time.

Treasured Reflections: You may not have had an experience like mine, but do you have a special friend—married, single, or widowed—who is your Godsent provision?

Treasured Thoughts: Journal your thoughts about widows who have comforted you in your mourning. It may seem far off, but can you anticipate, as you move along in your grief path, that God will use you to comfort others? Read 2 Corinthians 1:4. Are you a widow further along in your journey? How can you fill a void in another widow's life? God doesn't waste our pain nor does He waste our comfort.

"Having someone who understands
is a great blessing for ourselves.
Being someone who understands
is a great blessing to others."

Janette Oke, *The Father of Love*

25

Background Music

He has caused his wonders to be remembered;
the LORD is gracious and compassionate.

PSALM 111:4

Immediately after Doug proposed, he and my daughter Kate called to share the news: They were engaged! As I talked to them, I could hear the excitement in their voices. I too shared in their delight. When I hung up, despite the ache in my heart that my husband wasn't there to share the joy, I prayed God would give me smiles the minute they walked in the door. It had been three weeks since Randy went to heaven.

My husband's absence during the wedding planning was felt keenly. Randy and I had shared in wedding preparation for our other daughters. This time, I was doing it without him. Planning a wedding when you're recently widowed is difficult. Regardless of the delight in knowing your daughter has found the love of her life and God's man for her, I liken it to an amputee preparing his best friend for a track meet. There's joy in the other's achievement, but pain as you look at what you've lost. In a covenant marriage, two become one. As a new widow, I felt as if part of me had been amputated. After forty-two years and four months of marriage, it had.

Even with my daughter's help, I was making many financial decisions, making phone calls, and doing wedding research on my own. Randy wasn't there to see Kate model wedding gowns, give a nod of approval, and tell her she was beautiful. For that matter, he wasn't there to do the same for me as mother of the bride. His silence spoke loudly. Yet, from start to finish, God provided strength and people to help. Things fell into place quickly, and by March, plans were fully in place. On some days, I even felt joy.

The day before the wedding, we went to the venue to set up a photo display and centerpieces. After we finished, I was talking with the banquet manager when I heard my daughter Heather calling my name. I looked over and saw my daughter Susan crying. Heather and Kate's faces looked amazed.

"Listen," they said in unison.

I stopped my conversation and paused to listen. The song "Ashokan Farewell" was playing. "When have you heard that playing through a speaker?" Heather asked.

"Never," I said, shaking my head. "Ashokan Farewell" was the beautiful piano and violin duet Heather and Kate played to open their father's memorial service six months earlier. It was one of his favorite pieces.

"It's a benediction; a blessing," I said. "It's as if Dad is saying, 'I see. I know. I'm here.'"

It wasn't background music at all, but the treasure of my husband's presence.*

Treasured Reflections: What song or instrumental piece holds special meaning for you? Perhaps something that reminds you of your husband or marriage? Have you had the experience of hearing it on the radio or in a store, and you knew it was more than a coincidence? Does something else hold special meaning for you? One of my friends finds pennies in places she and her husband visited. She considers them a treasured reminder of his presence.

Treasured Thoughts: Journal your thoughts about song lyrics that speak to you. Perhaps it's a chorus or hymn you sing in church.

---

* You may want to listen to the beautiful "Ashokan Farewell." Only recently I discovered lyrics to the tune. They speak of love, treasured times, and farewell. My husband and I loved it, especially when performed by our daughters.

"He anticipates our crises. He is moved by our weaknesses. . . . And at just the right moment He steps in and proves Himself as our faithful heavenly Father."

Charles Swindoll, *Simple Faith*

26

Wedding Day Praise

Through Jesus, therefore, let us continually offer to God a
sacrifice of praise—the fruit of lips that openly profess his name.

HEBREWS 13:15

One of my husband's favorite musical compositions was *The Plan-
ets* by Gustav Holst. We often played it at home. Later, Michael
Perry wrote lyrics to accompany the "Jupiter" movement. "O God
Beyond All Praising" is a beautiful composition giving praise to God in
sorrow and in blessings. As a tribute to her dad, Kate decided to walk
down the aisle to this hymn. We also wanted to display God's unfailing
love to us and in our sorrow, offer praise and thanks.

Weeks prior to the wedding, Kate and I listened repeatedly to the
hymn in an attempt to desensitize ourselves so we wouldn't cry on her
wedding day.

In Isaiah 61:1–3, the prophet proclaimed the good news that God
had sent him to "bind up the brokenhearted, . . . to bestow on them a
crown of beauty instead of ashes, the oil of joy instead of mourning,
and a garment of praise instead of a spirit of despair. . . . They will be
called oaks of righteousness, a planting of the LORD for the display of
his splendor."

Incorporating my late husband into our daughter's wedding day
through his beloved music was a priceless treasure in our grief and a
testimony to the God we love.

We hoped we displayed God's splendor that day.

Treasured Reflections: One of my treasures has been listening to this
hymn and absorbing the meaning of the words. I don't cry like I used

to and now hear it with great joy. I praise God for His continued presence and healing. You can find the hymn sung by a choir online. Listen and be surrounded by the love and greatness of God.

Treasured Thoughts: Journal your thoughts about the lyrics from this hymn or another one that is meaningful to you.

27

Anchors

Truly my soul finds rest in God.

PSALM 62:1

One summer when my grandchildren came to visit, we went boating. We chose a spot to anchor, and the kids had a blast jumping off the boat and swimming. At one point, the boat seemed unstable, and we had to set the anchor again. I couldn't help but make a spiritual analogy to anchors and what they do and *who* my anchor is, especially in this life season with its uncertainties and newness.

Over the next few days, the concept of real anchors and stability appeared in several readings from different sources. It's something God wanted to impress on me for good reason.

Anchors moor or hold a boat in place and keep it from drifting. They are especially helpful if someone chooses to swim away from the boat. Swimmers need to know the boat is where they last left it. We can count on anchors. They're stable and reliable.

Hebrews 6:19 tells us, "We have this hope as an anchor for the soul, firm and secure." This hope, our anchor, is Jesus.

The sudden loss of my husband taught me much about anchors—or, rather, the real, immovable anchors of my life. My husband helped anchor me. With him, I felt secure and safe. His passing meant the end of certain dreams and plans for a long retirement together. Our forty-two plus years together were anchored but now moved.

People often say, "Don't look at your circumstances." But my circumstances are *real*. I live in them 24/7. I now pay the bills, take out the garbage, get the oil changed, eat meals alone, have no one to say "God bless you" when I sneeze or to fasten the clasp on my bracelet.

So I choose to live in two places at the same time: *in my circumstances* (there is no reversing them or getting away from them) and *above my circumstances* tied to my real anchor.

In Jesus I'm secure. He is the one who keeps me from drifting into negatively imagining my future and engaging in glum thoughts about my present. His promises are true and His love never-ending. He is faithful and is with me every minute of my day.

He is the one anchor who doesn't move. Stable, secure, immovable, and unchanging. He is my ultimate security and faithful anchor . . . always.

Treasured Reflections: Get to know your Anchor and His promises. Call out for His peace, comfort, and direction as you navigate in two places—in and above your circumstances. He will answer and provide treasures even in pain.

Treasured Thoughts: Journal your thoughts about living in two places and how your Anchor is present in both.

"Tears are the natural form of release for the still-suppressed feelings of love and gratitude, and also for the reservoir of pain and sorrow we have in our hearts. I have no doubt whatsoever they are God's gift to us in grief."

Zig Ziglar, *Confessions of a Grieving Christian*

Some Widows Say . . .

My friends and I admit that when we were married, we had no real understanding of what it meant or felt like to be a widow. Do any of the following statements reflect your thoughts now? You may want to voice some of these thoughts to a friend, but sometimes silence is best. Showing grace to others and praying that your hurt lessens is always a wise choice.

- Please talk about my husband. Use his name. Share a memory.
- Think before telling me about your latest dinner out at a fabulous restaurant with your husband, and please don't criticize and complain about him. I'd give anything to have mine back.
- I need to cry. Let me. God wired us to cry in sorrow and pain.
- I will do things when I'm ready. Your timetable is not mine. What another widow does or doesn't do is not my script. Just because she went on a cruise six months after losing her husband doesn't mean I should.
- It's my business when I decide to remove my wedding ring, remove his clothes from the closet, or sell his car.
- If you have not lost a husband, please don't tell me you know how I feel. You don't.
- If I tell you I feel that any minute my husband will walk through the door, I'm not hallucinating. I'm telling you the reality of his death hasn't sunk in yet.
- Don't tell me, "Let's get together," and then not call.
- Continue to invite me out. There are days I may not want to go, but there may be a day I do.
- My thinking is fuzzy; please be patient with me.
- I'm doing the work of two people, but I don't have forty-eight hours in a day. I don't want sympathy, just acknowledgment that

I'm adjusting to a different life . . . and maybe could use some help to get organized.

- Sometimes I'm tired and overwhelmed by the many unfamiliar decisions I need to make and tasks I must do. I have no one to talk over decisions with.

28

I Should Have Had a Plan

Anxiety weighs down the heart.

PROVERBS 12:25

In sweet and genuine gestures, friends invite us to social events. To their credit, they are attempting to get us out of the house and in the company of people we enjoy. Continued isolation isn't healthy. Our challenges come when we weigh the advantages of being with people versus being alone or being uncomfortable. Do you agree it's a balancing act?

Early in my loss, I was invited to a couples dinner. I didn't want to go. One of my daughters encouraged me to accept the invitation.

"It will be good for you. They love you and want you there."

Have you heard that? *It will be good for you.*

Reluctantly, I went. Yes, we loved each other. I'd known them for years. After nearly two hours, I wanted to leave but couldn't because I'd been given a ride. In another gracious offer, a couple picked me up to attend a holiday open house so I wouldn't drive alone. It presented the same scenario. After an hour and a half of conversation and laughter, I was ready to go home. But again, since someone else drove, I was captive.

I should have had better exit plans so I could leave on my timetable. Years later, it's not as important for me, but it may be something for you to consider. Weigh your choices and think of the better option: driving alone or with others. It's not driving to a destination or the arrival time that is important, but managing your departure when you know you're ready to leave.

I'm still not sure that the evening was "good" for me. On one level, it was difficult. On another, I use it to compare where I am now. I now

85

feel comfortable attending most events and can accept or decline invitations for transportation with confidence. We must start somewhere. I've made progress and am moving forward.

Treasured Reflections: How do you feel about attending social gatherings? The type and length matter, as well as who is attending, so give yourself freedom to choose and permission to decline. You might want to say, "I'll get back to you." Have you been in a similar situation where you wish you'd had an exit plan? Does it still matter?

Treasured Thoughts: Everyone is different, but a good barometer of healing may be your attendance at social events. Journal your reflections on how you've managed them. Do you find yourself a little less sensitive or are some events still difficult?

"Grief is not a disorder, a disease or a sign of weakness. It is an emotional, physical, and spiritual necessity, the price you pay for love. The only cure for grief is to grieve."

Earl A. Grollman, *Suicide*

29

Rocks and Boulders

The LORD is my rock and my fortress and my deliverer,
my God, my rock, in whom I take refuge, my shield,
and the horn of my salvation, my stronghold.

PSALM 18:2 ESV

I walked into my house after an evening with friends. I'd learned to keep lights on even if I left during daylight. Entering a house that's illuminated is a salve on the wound and pain of an empty house. My house is fully furnished. It's just that there's no other person occupying it or at home to greet me when I walk in. It's devoid of companionship.

I've been able to measure my progress in my grief journey when I walk into the house. As you may know, grief comes in waves. We progress but sometimes take a step backward. That night, I noted a step forward. I recalled the first time I'd gone to a neighbor's home for dinner after my husband's passing and returned to an empty house. It felt as if a huge boulder had moved from my throat, as I swallowed hard, to my stomach. It settled there. I burst into tears. I wondered if it was worth it—to go out, only to return to have that painful reminder that I am alone.

This time when I went out, I returned to the same empty house. But eight months later, there was a difference. This time, I felt a smaller rock, not a boulder. Still hard, but a little easier. God's grace helped me carry that heavy load. By the incremental change in the pit of my stomach, God showed me that His healing continues. Seeing progress was a treasure.

Treasured Reflections: If you've had that "boulder experience," be confident that God will help you carry it, and it will decrease in size. If that boulder has changed into a smaller rock, be thankful for progress and healing.

Treasured Thoughts: Journal thoughts about your progress in your grief journey.

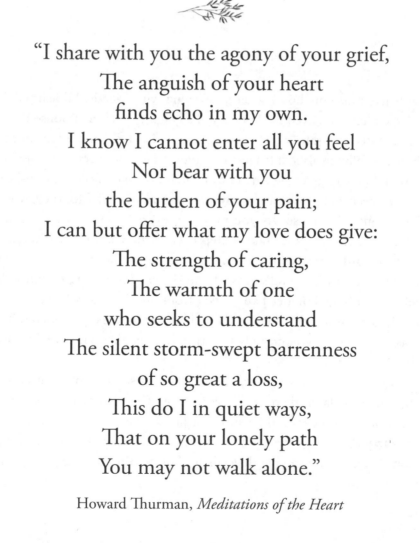

"I share with you the agony of your grief,
The anguish of your heart
finds echo in my own.
I know I cannot enter all you feel
Nor bear with you
the burden of your pain;
I can but offer what my love does give:
The strength of caring,
The warmth of one
who seeks to understand
The silent storm-swept barrenness
of so great a loss,
This do I in quiet ways,
That on your lonely path
You may not walk alone."

Howard Thurman, *Meditations of the Heart*

30

Walking Him Home

Even though I walk through the valley of the
shadow of death, I fear no evil, for You are with
me; Your rod and Your staff, they comfort me.

PSALM 23:4 NASB

In the beautiful song, "Walking Her Home," Mark Schultz describes a man's courtship, marriage, birth of a son, and the eventual death of his wife. In each season, he is at his wife's side.

One Sunday morning, several months after my husband went to heaven, my pastor used those lyrics to introduce his sermon from Genesis on the death of Sarah. Tears welled as I remembered the night my husband left earth for heaven. Unlike the character in the song, I didn't have the opportunity to say goodbye. We thought the stent procedure would remedy his problem and we would see him in a few hours.

The week following the sermon, I listened to an interview in which the guest said we often confuse God's protection with His rescue. No, God's protection is His *presence*. My antennae went up as I recalled prayers for my husband while the cardiac team worked on him. I prayed for the team's skill and accuracy, and for an unblocked artery and healing. I also prayed continuously that God would protect my husband.

Protection equals presence. God was present in the cardiac lab, and He was present over my husband's body. "Even though I walk through the valley of the shadow of death . . . You are with me." God was protecting my husband as he walked through the valley from earth to heaven. My prayers for protection were answered. Nearly eight months later, God revealed that though I hadn't been in the same room with Randy, I was walking him Home.

Treasured Reflections: Can you recall one treasured moment on the day your loved one left earth for heaven?

Treasured Thoughts: Journal your thoughts as you reflect on that day.

"Appropriate expressions of sorrow help move us through and beyond the grieving process. Express your feelings. Allow tears to flow. Share your sadness with others. Acknowledge your pain and tell your story. By honestly expressing your grief, you are taking an active role in God's plan for your recovery."

Criswell Freeman, *A Journey with God beyond Grief*

31

Gift Responses

Every good and perfect gift is from above, coming
down from the Father of the heavenly lights, who
does not change like shifting shadows.

JAMES 1:17

My dear friend Susan called me in the morning on my wedding
anniversary to see how my day was going. "Not the best day,"
I answered. "I've cried and thought a lot." She invited me to come to
her house for dinner or, if I'd rather not, she'd bring dinner to me.

"No," I answered. "I appreciate it, but I think today is a day I need
to be alone." She prayed with me and asked God to give me a gift.

Gifts. Normally my anniversary gifts would have been flowers or
dinner out. A few times, I also enjoyed the extravagant gift of a cruise,
an overnight at a bed-and-breakfast, or jewelry. How would God answer her request for a gift?

Earlier that day I posted a remembrance on Facebook. It was our
forty-third anniversary—or what would have been. Nicole, a sweet
young mom from church, commented, "I'm praying for you. Can't
wait to hug your neck."

I drove to the cemetery and put flowers from my husband's garden
on his gravesite. As I left the cemetery, "Alleluia," one of his favorite
songs, played. A gift. I decided I would do things my husband would
have appreciated. I went to Starbucks and used *his* card. Starbucks is
an unlikely place to experience a heaven-sent gift, unless you consider
a pumpkin latte at holiday time a gift. I'd just placed my order for my
decaf and low-fat mocha java chip when Nicole surprised me! She
grabbed my neck, gave me a big hug, and held me tight. She was my

first (and only) physical contact of the day. Referring to her Facebook comment, she said, "That's what I wanted to do!" She was a treasured gift to me sent from heaven. But I had to go to Starbucks to get it.

I left for a salon and had my eyebrows waxed. Not exactly pain-free, but it reminded me of how I always wanted to look nice for my husband. I cleaned the hardwood floors he liked (and I didn't want) in memory of shared experiences. Then I drove to our lake and sat in the sunshine, enjoying the calm water, blue Carolina sky, and the expanse of green trees we'd always enjoyed together.

I read Psalm 91 and played songs from one of our favorite Christian groups. I remembered attending their concert together and how we played their music repeatedly driving from North Carolina to visit our family in Pennsylvania.

It was a day of tears, memories, and gifts.

Later that day, I checked Facebook. I had twenty-eight comments and over seventy "likes" to my earlier Facebook post. As I sat at the screen, my oldest daughter's friend messaged me. "I viewed the photos Heather posted of your trip to see her a few days ago. You have never looked more beautiful," she wrote. "Your smile tells me God's grace gets us through any trial." *Grace.*

Before getting ready for bed, I checked email and heard from a dear friend telling me her husband had been diagnosed with melanoma and they were waiting for further biopsy results. The news took me by surprise. As I hit "reply," I wondered what I could possibly say that wasn't a platitude. I committed to pray and love my friend, to offer to be a listening ear.

Gifts, I thought, as I put my head on my pillow that night. Susan's prayer was answered. I received several gifts, and I gave one. Those memories also became gifts to myself.

Treasured Reflections: Before you rest your head on your pillow tonight, remind yourself of one gift you received today. Did you give one?

Treasured Thoughts: Journal about your treasures of pleasant, unexpected experiences and the Godsent people who were part of them.

"Having now spent more than forty-one years single, I have learned that it is indeed a gift. Not one I would choose. Not one many women would choose. But we do not choose our gifts, remember? We are given them by a divine Giver who knows the end from the beginning and wants above all else to give us the gift of Himself. . . . It is within the sphere of circumstances He chooses for us—single, married, widowed—that we receive Him. It is there and nowhere else that He makes Himself known to us. It is there we are allowed to serve Him."

Elisabeth Elliot (widowed twice), *Let Me Be a Woman*

32

From My Morning Room

In the beginning you laid the foundations of the earth,
and the heavens are the work of your hands.

PSALM 102:25

Each morning, I sit on my sofa with my Bible, books, and journal for quiet time. The coffee table is conveniently placed so I can reach my coffee mug and prop up my feet. It's a comfortable spot. The drapes are open, and I have a view of the birds and squirrels in our backyard. I have a front-row seat to changing seasons. The flowers boast assorted colors and sizes; the stately pine trees drop their needles, forming a blanket on the ground; the shrubs are both bright and deep green; and in winter, bare branches offer a new setting. It's a beautiful sampling of God's creation.

Did I mention it's the dream retirement home my husband and I built three years before he died?

Early in my loss, I felt compelled to reread Kay Arthur's book, *To Know Him by Name*. My husband had given it to me years earlier, but I wanted to get reacquainted with the character of God on my new path. The gift book contains beautiful drawings and lots of space to write down thoughts. My brain could handle the reading. The text conveyed meaning but was short enough to accommodate my cloudy brain.

The first chapter is devoted to *Elohim*, Creator God. That's the first name for God revealed to us in Scripture, and we meet Him in Genesis. It was fitting I started with that name as I meet Him every morning in a prime spot to view His creation. The beautiful blue Carolina sky is a canopy that reminds me He created the heavens and the earth and all that is in it. He also holds it all together—truth I desperately needed to remember.

In my grief, God spoke to me often about who He is as my Creator. Just as the bare trees in winter will blossom in spring, Elohim will not leave me (or you) bare in our grief. He works in our lives to help His daughters change and grow. He is always out to create something new in us.

Widow was a new status, and with it my perspective and life changed. Now I have new relationships out of new circumstances. The relationships my husband and I once shared with others are now different and, in some cases, gone. My mindset and attitudes are new and different. Even my daily agenda is different. I'm doing things I never did before, most out of necessity. Plans that were "our" plans as husband and wife have changed to "my" plans, singular plans, plans that were never on the radar. Our dream of a long, shared retirement was halted. Plans for "us" were deleted.

But Elohim, Creator God, chose to create something new. Some days it's a change of heart and attitude. Other days it's a new challenge or opportunity I never anticipated yet was able to accomplish. He has given me a grief and writing ministry. Sometimes He brings a new person into my life or uses a friend to encourage and enrich me. Some days I gain a new level of compassion for someone because of the compassion God has given me. I can reach out to a widow new in grief.

My status changed, but Elohim's did not. He remains my Creator God.

Each time He creates, it's a treasured moment, and I know He loves and holds me together.

Treasured Reflections: Step outside and bask in God's creation. Stop and thank Him for the beauty. The same Creator God sees you, holds you together, and is creating in you. Reflect on one thing you see today as God's creation in you since you've been widowed.

Treasured Thoughts: Journal the changes in you: What have you resisted that you now accept? What accomplishment has surprised you? How have you helped another widow or reached out in compassion to someone? Has hidden potential surfaced? Journal thoughts about

God's beauty in creation and the way He's recreating you. Does the beauty of changing seasons encourage you? Look at Psalm 138:8 and Colossians 1:17 as you reflect.

"Healing takes time and patience.
Healing requires hope, and we
must medicate ourselves with hope
daily; If necessary, even hourly."

Margaret Brownley, *Grieving God's Way*

33

What a Difference
a Year Makes

Weeping may last through the night, but
joy comes with the morning.

PSALM 30:5 NLT

On my first anniversary without my husband, I recalled how we'd celebrated our forty-second anniversary on an Alaskan cruise. Never in a million years did I think he wouldn't be around for our forty-third. I think I relived each day of that week, reminding myself of our itinerary and picturing what we did.

Following our cruise, I wrote a devotion for my website using some insights from our trip. I reread it that morning to remind myself of treasures.

"Don't miss the treasures," the lecturer said, "by comparing the cities you've come from with the land you'll see."

Now tears obscured the "treasures." My most treasured person was no longer with me. I compared where I was a year ago with where I was then. "We" shared treasures together. It's now "I."

But my grief journey, as yours, is not without treasures. There are people who come along at the right time to help with a home repair or give a hug. We experience personal growth because of something we've had to learn out of necessity. We survive a painful day, such as a birthday or anniversary. We read the exact Scripture that speaks to where we are or read a devotion with a profound truth we hang on to. We have a friend who prays with us. Like viewing Alaska's natural beauty, not one of the treasures I mentioned is a material one.

As I looked back and reflected on our trip, I saw many treasures. We had to look and wait, for example, in order to see humpback whales surface. Today will hold treasures too.

Treasured Reflections: Just for today, can you look in order to see? At the end of the day, think about what you found. Consider thanking God for five things as you rest your head on your pillow tonight. Make it a nightly ritual, and you will find treasures every day.

Treasured Thoughts: Journal your thoughts about what you see. What surprises you?

Gratitude List
There Is a Future and Hope

"For I know the plans I have for you," declares the
Lord, ". . . plans to give you hope and a future."

JEREMIAH 29:11

Every day holds something to be thankful for and to appreciate about your life. You might want to buy a journal just for a gratitude list, adding to it each day or week. When you do, you'll begin to see positive aspects of your life even as you mourn.

A while back, I began using a gratitude jar. I write something I am thankful for on a slip of paper and put it in a mason jar. At the end of the year, I dump out the slips of paper and read each one. It's amazing the things we forget. It is a gift to read and remember.

Another step of gratitude is also a sleep aid. When I rest my head on my pillow, I rewind my day and think of five things to be thankful for. Soon I'm asleep. Why not try it?

34

The Letter "H"

"Do not conform to the pattern of this world, but
be transformed by the renewing of your mind. Then
you will be able to test and approve what God's
will is—his good, pleasing and perfect will."

ROMANS 12:2

Quinn ran upstairs and proudly announced, "I learned about the letter 'h'!"

"What did you learn?" I asked.

"Well, the letter 'h' is a transformer," he answered.

"A transformer?" I questioned in surprise. I didn't expect to hear that word out of his five-year-old mouth. "What does that mean?" I probed.

"The letter 'h' changes sounds," he continued. "Like with 't.' If you put an 'h' next to a 't,' it becomes 'th.'"

"Oh!" I responded. "That's an interesting way to think about it—a transformer. Can you give me an example of a word?"

"Three," he answered, beaming. "It happens with 's' too," he said, smiling.

"How's that?" I asked. By this time, I was pleased he had retained the concept, and I could tell he was excited to share his new information.

"An 'h' next to 's' makes a 'sh' sound, like in 'shell.'"

"Super!" I said and gave him a high five. "It's fun to learn new things, isn't it?"

Satisfied he had shared his new knowledge, Quinn went back to the playroom. But our conversation lingered in my mind as I thought about the object lesson he'd given me. Transformers. Changes. Nothing transforms anyone more than losing a loved one. Life is irrevocably different.

My life will never return to what it was prior to December 23, 2011, when I lost my husband. But I have seen some positive transformations. I smile when the grandchildren speak of their Papa and the memories they made with him. I know, in some way, they've been transformed by his presence in their short lives.

Our youngest daughter married six months after her dad went to heaven. God blessed our family with joy and smiles on her wedding day as we celebrated her new beginning.

My husband was the gardener in our family, but now I weed his beautiful garden and try to preserve it as he would have. Working in the dirt has transformed me. I now have an appreciation of the work it takes to maintain beauty.

Life is different, and God is in my transformation. He gives me what I need to walk through each day, on the days of smiles with my grandchildren, on the lonely days, and on the challenging days.

Treasured Reflections: How have you seen moments of positive transformation during your grief journey?

Treasured Thoughts: Journal thoughts about your transformation in roles, tasks, and perspective.

"Grief is the constellation of internal thoughts and feelings we have when someone we love dies. Think of grief as the container. It holds all of your thoughts, feelings, and images of your experience when you are bereaved. In other words, grief is the internal meaning given to the experience of loss.

"Mourning is crying, talking about the loss, journaling, sharing memories, and telling stories. Other ways to mourn include praying, making things, joining in ceremonies, and participating in support groups. Mourning is how, over time, we begin to heal. It is through active and honest mourning that we reconstruct hope and meaning in our lives.

"It is essential to mourn your life losses openly and honestly, expressing your grief outside of yourself. Over time and with the support of others, to mourn is to heal."

Alan D. Wolfelt, *Understanding Your Grief*

35

Rock Collecting

He has made everything beautiful in its time. He has
also set eternity in the human heart; yet no one can
fathom what God has done from beginning to end.

ECCLESIASTES 3:11

Whenever it rained, water pooled in the low point of my neighbor's yard, soaking the grass. A retaining wall wasn't needed, but the landscaper suggested piling rocks in the area to slow the water flow and avoid standing water. After our usual three-mile walk one morning, my friend Lanette and I got into her car and drove around our neighborhood to look for rocks.

We scouted a couple of vacant lots and found rocks in different sizes, shapes, and even colors; enough to fill the trunk of her car. Her husband arranged them in the needed spot. Time will tell if that solved the problem.

Randy and I had done the same thing when we'd moved into our home three years earlier. We didn't need to stop runoff but wanted large decorative rocks. To this day, they enhance my yard, and I vividly remember sharing that time with my husband. We were retired and enjoying our new home in North Carolina. Little did I know we'd enjoy it together for such a short time.

I stared at the pile of rocks in Lanette's trunk. They looked like just a pile, but once placed in her backyard, they became an attractive and functional arrangement.

Thinking of those rocks—some big, some small, others sharp or smooth—made me think of my journey. There are the hard, heavy moments where waves of sadness come. Sometimes there are short, "smaller" moments when my eyes fill with tears, or I get a lump in my throat or a knot in my stomach. I feel my loss when I'm frustrated and tackle a project out of my skill set that resembles a random pile of rocks. Seeing couples holding hands is one of the sharpest rocks.

Other rocks are so big I can't move them. Those rocks are holidays and special occasions, where the loss is large, my heart is heavy, and everything else is obscured. There are other days when I have energy to go to lunch with a friend, spend time with my prayer group, or go to the beach with friends and even laugh.

Like rocks, some moments are sharp and have jagged edges that hurt. Others may be smoother, and I have a brief respite. The moments are all necessary and function together to move me forward on my grief and mourning path.

Grief experts remind us not to be stuck in our grief. I guess being stuck is much like leaving my grief "rocks" in the trunk of a car. When I saw how beautifully arranging them in the right place made a difference, it made a difference in me too. When I realized the rocks had functional value, I reminded myself that God has a purpose not only in my loss and grief, but for my *life*. As I heal, purpose emerges like the beautiful rocks in my front yard. God is accompanying me on my journey; the large, sharp, and hard moments combine with the smooth and smaller ones. In each "rock," I find *grace*.

Treasured Reflections: What are your small and big grief rocks? Where have you found a treasure in a rocky experience?

Treasured Thoughts: Journal thoughts about rocky experiences, knowing it took time to move the rocks from the field to the trunk of the car, and then to arrange them in the yard. Have some of those sharp rocks become smoother?

"As far as I can see, grief will never truly end. It may become softer over time, more gentle, but some days will feel sharp, but grief will last as long as love does—forever. It's simply the way the absence of your loved one manifests in your heart. A deep longing, accompanied by the deepest love. Some days, the heavy fog may return, and the next day, it may recede, once again. It's all an ebb and flow, a constant dance of sorrow and joy, pain and sweet love."

Lexi Behrndt, "How to Be Grateful When Life Is Hard"

36

It's in the Air

Yet this I call to mind and therefore I have hope: Because of the
LORD's great love we are not consumed, for his compassions
never fail. They are new every morning; great is your faithfulness.

LAMENTATIONS 3:21–23

The air was beginning to feel different. I recognized it as a signal
that summer was drawing to a close and school would start. Store
shelves that once held swim toys now displayed lunch boxes, note-
books, and school supplies. I knew stores rush seasons, but the change
in the air was unmistakable.

Already another season.

I remembered how much I dreaded the advent of spring. It meant
I was moving further away from when I last saw my husband in December. Summer brought the same reminder. Randy loved working in
the yard, and it showed. Neighbors walking past often stopped to tell
us we had the most beautiful yard in the community. So, as the flowers bloomed, summer wasn't nearly as hard. They were reminders that
brought a smile to my face. I got through spring and summer, but fall
was difficult. I was further and further away from that last December.
It was dark when I woke up in the morning, and it was damp and
chilly. I don't "do" that kind of weather well even in the best of circumstances. Fall marks more time spent inside alone. The next season
would mark a year.

When I spoke to my daughter Heather, she had the same uneasiness
about the change of seasons but offered some insight. The change of
seasons reveals the faithfulness of God. The seasons are predictable
and orderly.

"Imagine," she said, "if we didn't have seasons. We'd wake up and not know if it could be snowing, if leaves were falling from trees, or if it was 90 degrees and we could go swimming."

We laughed at the contrasts and imagined the chaos of preparing for an unpredictable day in terms of clothing and activities.

Just as with the weather, we go through seasons in our life. We marry, raise a family, become empty nesters and grandparents, and are widowed. Even though some life events come without warning and are unseasonable, God's grace and faithfulness meet us in each one.

Treasured Reflections: Do you have a difficult season coming up? Perhaps winter reminds you of a ski trip or summer speaks of vacationing at the beach. Each person copes and grieves in a different way. Can you be proactive and think of something you could do that might ease your pain? Perhaps you could invite an out-of-town friend to visit or plan a trip with friends.

Treasured Thoughts: Journal your thoughts about your grief in past seasons as you anticipate a new one.

37

Hard Saturdays

The LORD is close to the brokenhearted and
saves those who are crushed in spirit.

PSALM 34:18

Saturdays are some of my hardest days. Perhaps it's because they seem long, though they have just as many minutes and hours as the other six days of the week. I am not alone in thinking that way. Another widowed friend of mine expressed the same thought. Sundays are also difficult. Once you get home from church, the day is long and lonely. Sunday lunches with family gathered around your table or out with family at a restaurant are events of the past. Another friend says it's Friday nights for her . . . the traditional date night.

Why *does* it feel that way? On Saturdays, friends are busy with their husbands, and adult children are busy with Saturday errands or activities with their children. Other grandparents with grandchildren nearby are attending soccer or basketball games. The neighborhood seems quieter (or maybe noisier) as families are busy together. Saturdays are just plain hard . . . and long.

I thought about my Saturdays of the past. When my girls were growing up, Saturday was a morning to sleep in a little later and have, as my daughters called it, "a special breakfast." That breakfast might be pancakes, omelets, French toast, muffins, or cinnamon rolls. It was an opportunity for our family to leisurely sit at the breakfast table together and talk before getting on with Saturday chores or activities.

For years, our Saturdays were occupied with marching band and football games. We went to piano and violin recitals or school musicals. We joined other families for dinner (often at our home), and the adults talked while the kids played games or watched a movie. Soup or spaghetti sauce simmered on the stove, and the aroma permeated the air. I loved opening my home. Sundays were traditional family dinners, and Fridays were a night out or a movie at home with popcorn. After our daughters went away to college or left home, Saturday was a day for my husband and me to run errands and enjoy a calmer day together. He might work outside, and I inside, but we had companionship. Later we might go to dinner with friends or have people in.

Every widow I know agrees that Friday nights, Saturdays, and Sundays are now quite different. Like me, they're lonely without a companion.

Grief and mourning on weekends is a season in itself. My past active family- and friend- filled times were wonderful. I struggle to feel that way about my Saturdays now. Sometimes I run errands or complete household chores, but it's still hard. On Fridays, I will occasionally go out to dinner or a movie with other widows. We have a first Sunday of the month lunch bunch; and on other Sundays, my youngest daughter and her family come for lunch. Widowed friends started a Friday night Bible study to compensate for a date night. We began with ten; now we're up to twenty-two women. So we're working on making our weekends less difficult. When I put my head on my pillow at night, I'm thankful I made it through, and I know it's because of God's grace and the friendships He's provided.

Treasured Reflections: Are Friday nights, Saturdays, and Sundays hard for you? If you know other widows, can you brainstorm together to find solutions to lessen loneliness?

Treasured Thoughts: Journal thoughts about your loneliness. What could you do to lessen the pain? How might you reach out to someone who may be feeling the same way?

"We know that God knows our future and promises boundless hope. This doesn't mean we'll be spared pain, suffering, or hardship, but it does mean God will see us through that pain."

Jamie Tidd, *Leaning on God's Hope*

38

Close-up or Panoramic

Go after God, who piles on all the riches we could ever
manage—to do good, to be rich in helping others, to be
extravagantly generous. If they do that, they'll build a
treasury that will last, gaining life that is truly life.

1 TIMOTHY 6:17–19 MSG

Photos have taken on a life of their own in recent years. Gone are the days of having pictures developed, ordering double prints, and discarding half of them because they're out of focus. Today we take photos on our phones and upload to our computer. We delete, crop, change the tint, and eliminate red-eye. We filter photos to improve our appearance. We even take selfies.

One Thanksgiving, my son-in-law Paul took a panoramic photo with fifteen seated around the table. He sent the photo to me, and it replicated the occasion beautifully. If he had taken only a photo of individuals, a small group seated in the family room, or the host carving the turkey, he wouldn't have fully captured the event.

Do you think that happens in grief and loss? We can't help but focus on ourselves and our loss in the initial days and months of grief. Our life is dramatically changed. We can't escape it. Snapshots of our life have been cropped. The tint has changed. We can't remove the red-eye. It's as if we take selfie after selfie. But as months progress and we move into another year, we begin to see the larger picture. More scenery comes into view. We get into a routine. We may make new friends; some of our former friends move out of the picture. We move from being the only person in the photo to a larger scene.

Moving from selfies or individual snapshots to a panoramic photo takes time. Each widow responds according to her personality, opportunities, and circumstances. Wherever you are today, know more is waiting for you. Life will not be the same as it is now, and though different from the life you knew with your husband, the people and the scenery can hold beautiful treasures. There is more in the picture than you see now. More will come into view, and there will be more focus and less red-eye.

Treasured Reflections: If you're up to it, look through some photos and find a snapshot of a single person at an event and one that more closely depicts a panorama of the event. Use it as a visual reminder to take in the bigger picture of your life.

Treasured Thoughts: Journal your thoughts about the photos you found. Take a selfie and make notes about where you are today in your grief journey. Keep those notes handy and reread them in a few months.

"Trust God for the rest of the journey. He puts the rainbow at the end of the hardest trail."

Dale Evans Rogers interview, "Dale Evans' Faith Overpowers Pain"

39

New Paint

He who was seated on the throne said, "I am making
everything new!" Then he said, "Write this down,
for these words are trustworthy and true."

REVELATION 21:5

My husband and I wanted to move from neutral walls to color. Unfortunately, he went to heaven before we could do that together. After nearly a year, I decided I would get the downstairs painted and went on a mission with two friends to select paint colors. I admit I was in an approach-avoidance conflict. Part of me wanted to add some color to my home; the rest of me resisted change. My neighbor and I found a painter and got estimates. I was surprised when he told me he had the first week of December free. It became do or die. I did it.

The night before the painter came, I stared at blank walls and took a final look. My home had changed, and now my house was going to change too. In one and a half days, the lower level of my house was no longer a neutral off-white. I admit I love it. The almond cream/yellow added warmth, the bold red and brown in my study brought brightness, and the deep golden rust made the bathroom tile pop.

As my neighbor helped me put things in order, she reassured me that this was a good decision. "It's a new chapter," she said. I put my head on her shoulder and cried. She hugged me tightly. A necessary chapter was beginning, more change.

My friend Ann texted to see how things were progressing. I relayed in abbreviated text that it was hard and a permanent change for my remaining time in my house—another reminder that my husband was gone. She was knee deep in Christmas decorations, reluctantly decorating her home. She told me she had turned on praise music to help her, and I should do the same. I went to our CD player and pressed number two. My son-in-law Jonathan had given me several CDs of some of my husband's favorite music. Blasting through the speakers, I heard, "He makes all things new." I stood and absorbed it. The second piece rang out reminding me Jesus gives hope, rest, and grace to the weary. I was definitely weary. God again met me. Timely and perfect.

Supportive friends, recordings compiled months ago but needed for today, and splashes of color replacing sterile walls—all treasures.

Treasured Reflections: Listen to some praise music and let the treasures of truth wash over you.

Treasured Thoughts: Journal thoughts about changes you've made. Were they necessary, hard, welcomed, or . . . ? How would you describe the results?

"Can you imagine a world without the colour green? If overnight, the grass turned white, fields turned black, peas turned orange? That's a bit like grief: Overnight, our world looks different. A core colour is wiped out, and suddenly our landscape looks so very different."

Zoë Clark-Coates

40

It's Been a Year, Now What?

But for you who revere my name, the sun of
righteousness will rise with healing in its rays. And
you will go out and frolic like well-fed calves.

MALACHI 4:2

I went to Idaho for Christmas in 2012. Newlyweds Kate and Doug
flew in for a few days. Susan surprised us and showed up at Heather's house so she could be with us on December 23 to remember the
year anniversary of her dad's homegoing. We stayed busy, but I confess
my mind replayed every minute of December 23. We went to dinner at
my husband's favorite Mexican restaurant and remembered together.

I subscribed to GriefShare daily emails seventeen days after my husband died. Once back in North Carolina, I clicked on the email and
read "Day 365." I stared at the number, and though we had marked
one year of Randy's homegoing in December, seeing the number was
startling. I'd read 365 days of encouragement, Scripture, and illustra-
tions from others' experiences. Each greeted me on a different day and
in a different place on my grief journey. I cried on many of those days.

The last email encouraged readers to run to God and be encouraged
to grow forward. It also included an invitation to resubscribe and read
the emails again. I decided to do that. I thought the words would look
different if I reread them at a different stage of grief and mourning.
They did. I read and thought, *Yes, I've been there. But now I'm walking a different part of the path.*

Unlike an antibiotic prescribed for seven or ten days, the time and
methods for healing in grief do not have a prescription or timetable.

I know I'll never be *over* my loss, but I know I will continue to get through it and find life again, as will you.

Treasured Reflections: There are many books, websites, and devotionals on grief. Have you considered looking for one? Perhaps it will meet you where you are.

Treasured Thoughts: Have you hit your one-year anniversary? Journal your thoughts about living the past year alone. What hurts less now than a few months ago? What steps have you taken that you're proud of?

"Tuck [this] into your heart
today. Treasure it. Your Father
God cares about your daily
everythings that concern you."

Kay Arthur, *God, Help Me Experience More of You*

Spiraling
A Description of Grief

We experience grief differently. One person's way of handling it may resonate with us—we feel seen, heard, validated. Another person's approach may seem callous. Or excessive. Maudlin. Or detached. Do C. S. Lewis's words below describe your experience? What analogy would you use to describe your grief?

> For in grief nothing "stays put." One keeps on emerging from a phase, but it always recurs. Round and round. Everything repeats. Am I going in circles, or dare I hope I am on a spiral?
>
> But if a spiral, am I going up or down it? How often— will it be for always?—how often will the vast emptiness astonish me like a complete novelty and make me say, "I never realized my loss till this moment"? The same leg is cut off time after time. —C. S. Lewis, *A Grief Observed*

41

Caving In

Carry each other's burdens, and in this way
you will fulfill the law of Christ.

GALATIANS 6:2

North Carolina doesn't get much snow, but when we do, life stops. Malls, schools, and doctors' offices close, church services are cancelled. Winter 2014 brought an immobilizing accumulation of snow, even for me, who'd lived in New York and Pennsylvania most of my life.

One snowy evening at home, I heard a thump. Then another. I assumed it was snow falling from the roof. The next morning, I looked out to see the canvas canopy on my back patio had collapsed. Even the steel bracing had caved in. I cried when I saw it. My husband had put it up for us. We'd sat there to enjoy our morning coffee and many evenings together. It was another piece of him lost. I couldn't imagine how I'd tackle it.

I headed to the patio with a shovel and began breaking the snow and ice with a mallet, moving it to the backyard. The weight of the snow had torn much of the canvas canopy. I tore the remainder of the canvas for easier management—and to vent my frustration. My face was damp with falling snow and tears. I lugged the canvas and some of the broken steel into a pile for trash collection. Hours later, only the bolted braces remained. What a picture—an empty space where something special had been. Does that feel like life on some days?

My dear neighbors noticed what had happened and offered to remove the bolts with an electric drill. "I'd appreciate it, but no hurry. At your convenience," I told them gratefully.

Two days later, I received a text while I was walking into church. "The bolts are removed."

I shared my experience with my friend Linda, who sat next to me, and while we stood to sing, I said a silent prayer of thanks for neighbors and friends who were gifts to me in so many ways.

Sometimes when we feel we're caving in, God sends people to help us carry or remove our weights, even when it seems they're bolted down and immovable. That's what happened to me on that snowy January day.

Treasured Reflections: Have you had a weight lifted? Has someone been a treasured weightlifter for you?

Treasured Thoughts: Journal your thoughts about your weights and the changes you've seen.

42

Aching Arms

When Moses' hands grew tired, they took a stone and
put it under him and he sat on it. Aaron and Hur held
his hands up—one on one side, one on the other—
so that his hands remained steady till sunset.

EXODUS 17:12

Last night I heard a pastor speak at a venue an hour from my home. Before he began his message, he wanted to pray for those in the audience. He asked any who were undergoing a trial to raise their hands, and he would pray for them. I raised my hand.

The pastor prayed for trials by name: financial trials, job loss, rebellious children, illness, marital issues; the list continued. He prayed specifically with details for each category. He told us to keep our hands raised, knowing our arms would ache from the heaviness. He was right. I was distracted by the ache and wondered when he would get to my trial. He continued and continued. My arm hurt. He wanted us to release our burden as the ache increased.

My friend Susan was sitting next to me. She put her hand under my elbow and helped me keep my arm up. I thought of how Aaron and Hur held up Moses's arms, ensuring the Israelites gained victory in the battle. Susan did that for me.

My circumstances haven't changed, but my burden of discouragement and thoughts about my future have. God is at work. Grief is a process, and releasing doubts and discouragement in our unique way is part of the process. The pastor's prayer of intercession for a woman he didn't know was taken to the throne of grace as my sweet friend Susan held up my arm.

Treasured Reflections: Do you have a prayer you need to lift up to God to diminish your heartache or lessen your disappointment?

Treasured Thoughts: Journal your thoughts about someone who has held up your arms. File it away so one day you can do that for someone else.

"Sometimes all you can do is hug
a friend tightly and wish that their
pain could be transferred by touch to
your own emotional hard drive."

Richelle E. Goodrich, *Making Wishes*

43

Sensational Renewal

Ears that hear and eyes that see—the LORD has made them both.

PROVERBS 20:12

When my house went on the market, my realtor gave suggestions to improve the likelihood of a sale. Research indicated that flowering plants outside the entrance, and soft music and pleasant aromas in the home would enhance buyer appeal. A friend suggested I bake bread an hour before a showing, or, if that wasn't possible, to heat vanilla extract in a pan in the oven. I admit I tried those things, and when I returned after being out, even I wanted to buy my house.

Stimulating the senses is nothing new. Children love to come home from school to the aroma of freshly baked cookies. We walk into a pizzeria, and our mouth waters. In recent years, aromatherapy—using natural oils extracted from flowers, bark, and other parts of plants to enhance our sense of well-being—has become popular. Lavender calms us and peppermint energizes. Articles report we can change our neurochemistry by stimulating our senses.

Practically speaking, we can do this as part of our day.

See: Open your shades and blinds to let in sunlight. Look at the natural beauty around you—blooming flowers, birds at a feeder, or lightly falling snow. Add splashes of color in your home—even something as simple as a decorative soap dispenser.

Smell: Do you bake, burn scented candles, or have diffusers in your home? Treat yourself to some fragrant flowers.

Taste: What flavors do you enjoy? An herbal tea, black or flavored coffee, chocolate, popcorn, or swirling a piece of candy in your mouth?

Touch: This is one of the things widows miss most. I miss my morning hug and kiss. I mentioned to a friend that, since I rise early, the sunrise is my morning kiss. Planting a garden, rain or snow on your face, the covering of a soft blanket, hugging a friend, holding your grandchild's hand or another's hand in prayer, soaking in a hot tub or a shower, and furry friends all help to fill this void.

Hear: Some people are refreshed by music and others by silence. A phone call to or from a family member or friend, bird songs, and other sounds in our environment call to our sense of hearing.

God gave us our five senses. We can use them to refresh our soul and enhance our life. Most of the time, it's free.

Treasured Reflections: Which sense do you most identify with? What can you do to enhance your outlook and stir your senses?

Treasured Thoughts: Journal the way you've energized your senses and how you felt as a result. Make a note to remind yourself to do the same for others.

"Gratitude. More aware of what you have than what you don't. Recognizing the treasure in the simple—a child's hug, fertile soil, a golden sunset. Relishing the comfort of the common—a warm bed, a hot meal, a clean shirt."

Max Lucado, *Chronicles of the Cross*

44

Puzzle Pieces

And a little child will lead them.

ISAIAH 11:6

My grandson Levi dumped the puzzle pieces on the table. "That's a lot of pieces," I commented.

"Yes, one hundred," he answered. "One of the pieces is missing, but I'm going to do the puzzle anyway."

I watched him work, and when I walked over to see the finished product, I couldn't tell that a piece was missing. "You found all the pieces?" I asked.

"No, Nonni, right here," he said, pointing to the spot in the center of the puzzle. The dark wood of the table blended with the puzzle to obscure the missing piece. I congratulated him on his work and walked back to my chair, thinking how he offered me a treasured moment—not only in his company and enthusiasm, but also in the concept of puzzles.

I *am* puzzled. I never thought I'd be living my script as a widow at my age. I have lots of puzzling pieces to put together—yesterday it was car maintenance. Some people think I have more flexibility living a solo life (ugh!), and have lots of extra time, because I need only think about me. The opposite is true. I now do everything, making up for the missing piece of my husband. My widowed friends say a personal assistant would help!

When the children of Israel first gathered manna, they asked each other, "What is it?" (Exodus 16:15). They'd never seen this substance from heaven. There was just enough food to nourish them each day. God knew exactly what He was sending and how much they needed.

I hold up my puzzle pieces and often ask, "What is this? What's it all about? What do I do now, and how do I do it?" My script is unexpected and unfamiliar to me but known to God. It was heaven sent.

Yes, Levi, one of the pieces is missing, but we still work on the puzzle.

Treasured Reflections: What puzzle piece are you holding today? The Bible says, "God is able to bless you abundantly, so that in all things at all times, having all that you need, you will abound in every good work" (2 Corinthians 9:8). It's a promise for you.

Treasured Thoughts: Journal thoughts about the puzzle pieces of your life and how they are taking shape.

"Healing requires trusting God with all the pieces of a broken heart."

Margaret Brownley, *Grieving God's Way*

45

Backdrops

See what great love the Father has lavished on us, that we
should be called children of God! And that is what we are!

1 JOHN 3:1

I received some exciting writing news. Initially, I squealed in delight,
but within seconds reality hit. My husband was not there to share
my joy. Exuberance became a settled stillness, and the words resonated in my mind, *This time you'll experience it alone.*

I shared with a friend, also a widow, how everything seems to be
placed against a backdrop of loss and grief. Whether it's joy, disappointment, plans, holidays, or important news, all are placed against
the picture of loss.

One definition for *backdrop* is the painted cloth or picture that
serves as scenery or setting for a stage. Another definition is simply
"background." For a new widow, the backdrop for her life is often
grief or loss. The setting is different: There's no one to share news or to
celebrate (or recognize) an accomplishment. You sit alone in church,
and you no longer attend certain events and activities, being the odd
number in a gathering. The backdrop for your life is obvious.

Then it hit me as I showered. (I get a lot of revelations in the shower.)
Perhaps I can embellish the irreversible backdrop. Perhaps I should
add the backdrop of God's love. It was His love that welcomed my
husband home, has surrounded me with His presence, and provided
everything I've needed and more. Unconditional, always present, unchanging *love.*

The backdrop of loss is permanent, but so is God's love. His love
changes the focus of the scene, and other images emerge and come to life.

Treasured Reflections: What's your backdrop today? Regardless of the freshness of your grief or its longevity, God's love is there. Clinging to the truth of His unfailing love will make the difference in your focus.

Treasured Thoughts: Journal thoughts about your backdrops and how they're changing your perspective.

46

Frosted Glass

When Jesus spoke again to the people, he said, "I am
the light of the world. Whoever follows me will never
walk in darkness, but will have the light of life."

JOHN 8:12

When Randy retired, we relocated to a lake community in North
Carolina, expecting to enjoy many retirement years together.
We chose the house model, siding color, light fixtures, floor coverings,
and shrubs. We dealt with details, like the window in the bathroom. It
was clear glass and, in our opinion, very "public" for a bathroom that
overlooked the driveway. What were the designers thinking? We asked
that the glass be treated or frosted, and it was. I still hung blinds over
the window, but the frosted glass let light it.

Just shy of three years later, God called my husband home to heaven.
My life in our beautiful community changed. A walk with my husband
became a solo walk or a walk with a friend; Randy fishing on the dock
while I read a book became my walk to the dock and sitting at the lake.

As I stood in the bathroom, I saw an object lesson in the glass. While
our plans and dreams were clear, my path and plans were now frosted
and less clear. Our dream house was on the market. What was next?

Looking back two years after my husband's death, I wondered where
the time went and how I got through unknown territory frosted by
change, loss, and grief. Yet, light comes through even frosted glass. I've
experienced the light of God's Word to sustain me, the light of His love
to comfort me, and the light from friends who have accompanied me.

Life will never return to what it was, but each beam of light through
frosted glass reminds me there is more to step out and see.

Treasured Reflections: Are you looking through frosted glass? The light of God's love and wisdom shines through. Your path is now different, but His light is available for each day. Step out and access it.

Treasured Thoughts: Journal your response to the reflections above. How has the light of God's love helped you when your life seemed clouded with loss? Consider writing down your prayers for direction on specific matters.

"One sees great things from the valley, only small things from the peak."

Father Brown in *The Innocence of Father Brown* by G. K. Chesterton

47

Secondary Gains

Fear not, for I am with you; be not dismayed, for I am
your God; I will strengthen you, yes, I will help you,
I will uphold you with My righteous right hand.

ISAIAH 41:10 NKJV

Fourteen months into widowhood, I took the plunge and attended a writers' conference. I drove two hours alone to the venue and roomed with a writer I didn't know. As we got acquainted, we shared our family status. Her husband didn't take an interest in her writing, and she was in an unhappy marriage. She was interested in my grief journey and loved that my late husband had encouraged my writing.

People think widows have a single loss. But they don't. There are hundreds of losses and layers—those present and those that are future.

I shared that because my husband died six months before our daughter's wedding, his absence was a huge secondary loss. And because he took such good care of me and assumed responsibility for doing so many things, I'm in unknown territory. And there would be future losses, such as not sharing in the birth of grandchildren and other milestones.

"Have you ever thought of looking at secondary gains?" she asked.

"Secondary gains? Hmm. I hadn't thought of that."

At twenty-seven months since Randy's passing, I continued to think about it.

I supposed it was like looking at a glass as half full, making lemonade out of lemons, or of redeeming a bad situation.

I've had many secondary losses since that conversation—the addition of four grandchildren without my husband to share the joy was among my most profound. I will have future secondary losses until I go to my grave. Her comment led me to think about secondary growth I had (and will have). So, I began a list.

In grief, I managed to plan a wedding within a budget without my husband's business expertise and emotional support.

I discovered I can research and interview real estate agents to list my house.

I can get quotes and arrange for window cleaners, power washers, and painters.

I can deal with computer glitches—or at least know how and where to get help.

I can drive three hundred miles alone over roads I had never traveled to see a friend. I've learned the timeline for auto maintenance.

I can assemble a table for my foyer.

I can sit in a gathering with happily married people as the only single woman with much less grief.

I can learn—and have learned—to do things I've never done before.

All this is part of God's healing and restoration process. He's creating new things in my life. I didn't do any of it on my own. It's seeing the "I can" become real because His enabling strength moves my feet and His grace holds my hand. "For I can do everything [He calls me to do] through Christ, who gives me strength" (Philippians 4:13 NLT).

Do I wish I didn't have to do certain things? Of course. Invention and creativity are born out of necessity. So is putting one foot in front of the other. Because my primary loss is irreversible, my secondary losses continue. So will the growth and the gains.

Treasured Reflections: Have you made a list of secondary growth and gains? You may think you're standing still or moving backwards, but making your list will encourage you to see your growth. Beyond that, knowing Christ is the source of your strength, not just a resource, will bring comfort.

Treasured Thoughts: Journal about your secondary growth. What positive changes do you see? Does the list surprise and encourage you?

Changes and Growth

Grief and loss change us in immeasurable ways. Perhaps you *now know* how to pump gas, file taxes, make your airline reservations, buy tires, plant a garden, or change filters, and you couldn't do those things before. Make a list. You will be encouraged at how much you are growing and changing in positive ways. The list will give you strength and courage as you see your growth cataloged, and it will encourage you to help other widows on their path.

48

Lifting and Leaving

Because of the LORD's great love we are not consumed, for his
compassions never fail.
They are new every morning; great is your faithfulness.

LAMENTATIONS 3:22–23

Widowhood brings new decisions, and one of mine was to put my
house on the market. My newly married daughter had moved
out of state, and I had no family left in North Carolina. Like every
significant decision widows make, relocating is an individual matter.
Widows vary in when they decide to remove their wedding ring, clear
a closet of their husband's clothes, or sell his car. Some widows choose
to stay put; others downsize quickly. I prayed and waited about a year
before I decided to move.

My realtor arranged for a stager to tour my house and see what to
move and adjust so buyers would see my home in the best light. She
moved the angle of a carpet in my half bathroom (an interesting detail
that made a difference), removed curtains to let in more light, shifted
decor so the eye went to the right place, and recommended I clear out
a closet to reduce clutter.

I got to work on the closet. I sorted and purged; packed things in bins
and boxes and made two trips to a thrift shop. I rented a storage unit,
loaded my vehicle, and moved boxes into a climate-controlled unit.

Looking, thinking, lifting, moving, giving. It was tiring but proved
to be a good exercise for me.

The closet looked better. I felt better, optimistic my house would
sell and God would move me to the right house near my youngest

daughter, in His timing. I often see the application of spiritual truths from object lessons in everyday living. This was one of those times.

Widows know that widowhood is more than grief over a husband's death. From day one, our weights vary: decisions without the benefit of shared wisdom, new choices, the need for new skills, fatigue, financial adjustments, new friendships, not "fitting in" in former couples activities, loneliness, change. No two widows face their new life in the same way. Circumstances, marriages, and personalities are unique, but it is safe to say that "change" is a label that applies to each woman. Sometimes it's overwhelming.

So, I got to work, packed boxes, loaded my vehicle, and drove to the storage unit. I punched in the code to enter and open the gate. I unlocked the first door, unloaded, and took the boxes to my unit. I turned the key on the padlock and stacked my boxes. I pulled down the door, locked the unit and the exit door, got into my vehicle, used the access code to exit, and drove away. It was a process, one I'd never experienced before.

I made several trips, and the house looked lighter. I felt productive and, despite muscle soreness, I accomplished my goal.

That evening I rested and reflected on my day.

I saw a parallel to my widowhood journey as I remembered the Scripture passage: "Come to me, all you who are weary and burdened, and I will give you rest. Take my yoke upon you and learn from me, for I am gentle and humble in heart, and you will find rest for your souls. For my yoke is easy and my burden is light" (Matthew 11:28–30).

If I wanted my house to sell, I had to present it in the best light. That meant adjusting and following the recommendations of the stager and realtor. In a sense, they invited me to "come" and "take" their suggestions and "learn" the best way to present my house to others.

Now with some rearrangement and reduced clutter, it's the same house, but it looks different.

The Lord invites us to "come" and "take" our burdens to Him; to spend time and "learn" from Him and find His rest.

Our widowhood journey is a process of looking, thinking, lifting, moving, and giving. We often take two steps forward only to take one or two backward. Sometimes we push hard because our emotional, physical, or mental energy is nearly depleted.

When I come, take, and learn, God gives me focus. The burdens are lighter when I give them over to His wisdom and care, and His faithfulness is my companion. I'm the same house but I look different. I have more light.

Treasured Reflections: How can you apply Jesus's invitation to come, take, and learn?

Treasured Thoughts: What does the invitation to come, take, and learn look like for you? Journal your thoughts.

"Your greatest ministry will likely come from your deepest pain."

Rick Warren, "The Best Use of Your Deepest Pain"

49

Parts and Pieces

In their hearts humans plan their course, but
the LORD establishes their steps.

PROVERBS 16:9

My neighbor Judy pulled into my driveway one afternoon to stop and chat for a few minutes. She asked if I wanted to come to her house that night with our friend Linda to watch an episode of *Downton Abbey*.

"Sure," I answered.

"Great! 7:00," she responded. "See you then."

Later, the three of us sat in her kitchen catching up. One topic led to another, as we caught up on the "many parts and pieces to our lives," as Judy called it.

We talked about our adult children who lived out of town, our grandchildren, retirement and relocation, and my life alone. As the hours clicked away, and we reflected on life changes, we forgot all about watching *Downton Abbey*. At 10:00 p.m., we called it a night and said, "Another time."

I met Judy, Linda, and their husbands when Judy invited us to dinner three weeks after Randy and I moved into the neighborhood. They were new too. We clicked, and that evening evolved into a quarterly supper club where we took turns hosting. Linda and her husband were the couple who met us at the airport when Kate and I returned to Charlotte after Randy passed. Judy and Bob have made trips from Charlotte to visit me. We regularly stay in touch. And when Judy's husband died, I went to visit her and Linda joined us for lunch.

These friends became some of many parts and pieces of my life that still significantly fit. I call them treasures.

Treasured Reflections: Have you thought about the "parts and pieces" that fit together as grace and treasures?

Treasured Thoughts: Journal your thoughts about the moving and stationary parts of your life in your new path.

"*Never lose an opportunity of seeing anything beautiful.* Beauty is God's handwriting—a wayside sacrament; welcome it in every fair face, every fair sky, every fair flower, and thank for it *Him*, the fountain of all loveliness, and drink it in, simply and earnestly, . . . a cup of blessing."

Parson Lot (Charles Kinglsey), "The National Gallery—No. I" in *Politics for the People*

50

Wearing Glasses
on My Head

We don't yet see things clearly. We're squinting in a fog, peering
through a mist. But it won't be long before the weather clears
and the sun shines bright! We'll see it all then, see it all as clearly
as God sees us, knowing him directly just as he knows us!

1 CORINTHIANS 13:12 MSG

Six of my grandchildren live hundreds of miles away, so FaceTime is
a regular way to connect. One day, five-year-old Addy decided to
play with her glasses while talking to me. She moved them down on
her nose, and I mimicked her for fun.

"Hmm," I said. "That would not be very comfortable if we did it
all the time."

With a big smile, she moved them onto her head, and I followed suit.

"Well, that's worse! I can't see very well," I said, laughing. "Can
you see?"

"No," she agreed, giggling.

We moved our glasses to where they belonged and continued our
conversation.

I can't see very well. That's fresh grief in a nutshell. My eyesight
didn't change. The weather didn't bring fog. I wasn't driving with
swishing windshield wipers trying to keep up with pouring rain or rap-
idly falling snow. Grief changed my vision. It was as if I were wearing
glasses on my head. Hit with the unexpected death of my husband two
days before Christmas, I couldn't see well. It was only through God's
grace and the prayers of many that we went through the motions of

opening gifts with my grandchildren on Christmas morning. The days that followed—planning a memorial service and entering what some refer to as a "new normal" is much like wearing glasses on your head. I simply couldn't *see*.

Charting unknown territory—finances, auto care, computer glitches, household maintenance—the unfamiliar things my husband did, called for vision adjustment. So did trying to figure out my purpose. As the months passed, I had to move the glasses—from my head to my nose. But I often placed them too far down my nose. Anticipating and fulfilling certain tasks was blurred; so was life. I often needed to adjust my glasses.

I began to move my glasses with the support of friends and family, the accomplishment of formerly unfamiliar tasks, and through not being afraid to ask for help. Asking for help was humbling, but it was part of my vision adjustment. Slowly, God adjusted my vision. As the unfamiliar became familiar, my vision became clearer. There are times I still don't see clearly, but God has patiently accompanied me and given me the strength and wisdom I've needed to move forward.

Treasured Reflections: Does "wearing glasses on your head" sound familiar? What helped you move your glasses from your head to your nose?

Treasured Thoughts: Journal your response to your vision adjustment. One day you may be able to use your thoughts and process to help someone else.

"Change the way you look at things and the things you look at change."

Wayne W. Dyer, *The Power of Intention*

51

Dinner Invitation
and an Empty Chair

All my longings lie open before you, Lord;
my sighing is not hidden from you.

PSALM 38:9

Has it happened yet? You're invited to dinner at a friend's home and couples are seated around the table. You're the odd number. Years later, I vividly remember my first experience as if it were yesterday. As if being solo in a couples world isn't bad enough, being seated at a table next to an empty chair is downright painful. *Why couldn't someone sit next to me?* I thought. I tried to ignore the empty chair, but how do you do that when you need to stretch to pass the vegetables around the table?

I ate a meal, though I can't remember the menu. We talked, but I don't recall the conversation. I do remember the empty chair. When I returned home, I sighed. "Glad that's over," I muttered, thinking about the empty chair. As I got ready for bed, I evaluated the experience. My friends were loving and kind; it wasn't being a single with couples that bothered me as much as being placed next to an empty chair. The emptiness was glaring—literally and figuratively.

Laying my head on my pillow, I was thankful I'd gotten through it, like so many other firsts on my grief path. The experience prepared me for the next time, because there were going to be many "next times."

God's grace met me then. It promises to meet me each time; and with each meeting, there will be less pain—even when I sit next to an empty chair.

Treasured Reflections: How was your first experience at a couples dinner or event? Did you see the treasures of experience and grace get you through?

Treasured Thoughts: Journal your thoughts about the part experiences play in your grief journey, especially how you've changed from first-time experiences to now. Do you see fewer stings of hurt and more moments of grace, growth, and patience? Psalm 147:3 says, "He heals the brokenhearted and binds up their wounds." It's an ongoing process, not an overnight experience. How do you see that verse becoming real for you?

52

Via Points

No one is cast off by the Lord forever. Though he brings grief,
he will show compassion, so great is his unfailing love.

LAMENTATIONS 3:31–32

I am directionally challenged and rely heavily on my GPS. I often make two or three stops when I run errands on a single day. I choose the order of travel, and once everything is set, the first stop comes up as, "Set as a via point."

Never in a million years did I expect to be a widow in my sixties. My husband and I had plans to travel for fun and to see grandchildren, drink coffee on the patio, actively serve in our church, enjoy retirement, and grow old together. God chose otherwise. My marriage wasn't interrupted. It was terminated. We had fulfilled our vows to one another, till death do us part. My husband went home to heaven; and I'm here, currently in the via points of mourning, loss, living life alone, and in an unexpected detour to find purpose and hope.

Into my second year, the loss was glaring and permanent, but the grief had lessened and the navigation of a new normal continued with new experiences. Though humanly speaking I viewed my husband's death as an unnecessary stop, God wasn't wasting my via point of grief. He was working in my life through His faithfulness and His new mercies every morning. Since then, I've been able to encourage other widows and be a friend in their loss. Each challenge, new experience, new friend, and new grace is a via point I see with fresh eyes until I too go home.

Treasured Reflections: Where are you in your via point of grief? Don't rush it, but guard against getting stuck. Look for new experiences. God's mercies accompany you at each step as you move forward in His way and His time.

Treasured Thoughts: Journal your response to your via points. What do you see—a scenic route, detours, rest stops?

"When you start using senses you've neglected, your reward is to see the world with completely fresh eyes."

Barbara Sher & Barbara Smith, *I Could Do Anything If Only I Knew What It Was*

53

Laughter

A cheerful heart is good medicine, but a
broken spirit saps a person's strength.

PROVERBS 17:22 NLT

I remember the first time I genuinely and heartily laughed after my husband died. It struck me as odd—an emotion vaguely familiar but one not experienced in a long time. It felt strange. I was bewildered, wondering if this was the beginning of healing. At the same time, I felt a bit guilty and thought perhaps I'd betrayed my husband.

Since that time, I've had many occasions to laugh. Laughter is part of life. Though I live the reality of loss, it's different from fresh grief or self-pity. I have come to recognize the difference and guard my mind and heart if I slip into the kind of thinking that's not emotionally or mentally healthy.

This morning, during a phone conversation with my friend Ellen, she told me she was researching for a presentation on jokes. "Jokes?" I asked.

"Yes, good, clean, and even corny jokes. It's a presentation for a group of senior citizens. I subscribe to a Christian humor site, and I get jokes each week. Let me read some to you."

She proceeded to share some amusing riddles. She was right. They were corny, but I had to use some brain cells to come up with the answers, and each time we had a good laugh.

Laughter is not betrayal; it's good medicine.

Treasured Reflections: What do you think about laughter? Perhaps you'd like to subscribe to a site as my friend did and get a dose of medicine each week.

Treasured Thoughts: Journal thoughts about healthy laughter in your life.

"A good laugh is sunshine in a house."

William Thackeray, "On Love, Marriage, Men, and Women" in *Miscellanies: Prose and Verse*

54

Relocating

Wait for the Lord; be strong and take
heart and wait for the Lord.

PSALM 27:14

During the past year, two of my daughters sold and bought houses.
I did the same. My house was on the market for fourteen months.
I changed realtors, lowered the asking price, and took down family
pictures. I moved from a spring listing, to summer, then fall. Pleading in
prayer, I said I didn't want to return to my house after being away with
family at Christmas and start the new year in North Carolina. That
prayer was answered with no. January found me at the same address.

I had many house showings, but the objections dealt with things
I couldn't control: "We really wanted a ranch." My house was two-
story. "We wanted a big back yard for a pool." Mine was a small yard
with low maintenance and lots of trees. My life was interrupted with
showings, hopes dashed, and feeling as if I lived in a sterile museum.

My friend Jan, who lived down the street, had her house on the market too. We prayed our houses would sell, encouraged each other like
"iron sharpening iron," and lamented showings that came up empty.
We waited. My new realtor brought in a stager who made minimal
changes and said I'd done an excellent job preparing the house to sell.
So that wasn't the reason for the delay. God disregarded all of it, or so
I thought. He had other plans in mind, which became apparent as the
weeks and months passed.

When I finally received my only offer, I accepted it and found another house close to my daughter and her family in a neighboring state.
The purging and packing continued. I was profoundly thankful for an

army of help from my church. Moving day came; the truck was loaded. Neighbors stopped by and shed tears. Alone in my house, I took a final walk through and thanked God for the moments He gave us/me there. I took a photo of the empty great room—now a shell—where my husband often sat on a loveseat with his laptop or next to me watching a movie; where our grandchildren played games and our family laughed and talked. I sent the photo of the empty room to my girls. I was surprised I didn't sob.

Once I relocated, I found a new church, made friends, and even had a speaking invitation at a local church. The picture of my waiting came into focus. God was getting *me* ready to move. In His design, it wasn't about finding a buyer for my house or finding the right house in my new town (which turned out to be the perfect choice); it was about my being emotionally, relationally, physically, and mentally ready to move. It was about removing pictures from my home and changing furniture arrangements so that my house became less personal and easier to leave. Later, I came to see the principle of Isaiah 60:22 (NLT): "At the right time, I, the LORD, will make it happen."

Waiting is not doing nothing. It is an important something. I am thankful God waited for the right time. I look back now at the experience as a priceless treasure.

Treasured Reflections: Is a delay or denial in your life stressing you? Are you waiting and impatient for something to happen? Be thankful and rest in God's perfect plans. Psalm 27:14 is true.

Treasured Thoughts: Journal your responses to waiting.

"[God] is with us in the midst of our daily, routine lives. In the middle of cleaning the house or driving somewhere in the pickup. . . . Often it's in the middle of the most mundane task that he lets us know he is there with us."

Michael Card, *Joy in the Journey through the Year*

55

Life Events

There is a time for everything, and a season for every activity
under the heavens: a time to be born and a time to die, a time to
plant and a time to uproot, a time to kill and a time to heal, a
time to tear down and a time to build, a time to weep and a time
to laugh, a time to mourn and a time to dance, a time to scatter
stones and a time to gather them, a time to embrace and a time
to refrain from embracing, a time to search and a time to give
up, a time to keep and a time to throw away, a time to tear and
a time to mend, a time to be silent and a time to speak, a time
to love and a time to hate, a time for war and a time for peace.

ECCLESIASTES 3:1–8

My friend Susan was present during the birth of her grandson. Unfortunately, her husband was working out of state and couldn't see the newborn until days later. In our conversation, Susan revealed how sad she felt driving home alone because her husband wasn't there to share in the joy.

"I thought of you as I cried," she said, "and that you must feel that way at every major life event."

True.

I'd gotten through my daughter's wedding day with a smile and cried tears of release the next morning. Nearly two years later, her son was born. It was an exhilarating experience to kiss my daughter and hold my grandson. But yes, it was mingled with sadness at not sharing this moment with my husband. A few months earlier, I'd gone to court to witness my daughter Susan and her husband, Jon, officially adopt two boys. Once again, my husband wasn't there to share the joy.

The aunt of a close friend of mine advised her during a devastating loss: "Life changes. Get used to it." In a way, she was echoing Ecclesiastes 3. Life changes, and life happens. We shouldn't be surprised. Our feelings shouldn't surprise us either. There's a time to weep and a time to laugh. A time for everything. We accept and we respond, sometimes with tears and struggle as we hang on to God.

Treasured Reflections: What part of Ecclesiastes 3 are you experiencing?

Treasured Thoughts: Journal your response and thoughts about the "times" in your life Ecclesiastes describes.

56

Stepping Forward

Have I not commanded you? Be strong and courageous.
Do not be afraid; do not be discouraged, for the LORD
your God will be with you wherever you go.

JOSHUA 1:9

Friends from Pennsylvania were traveling south and stopped to visit for a few hours. Over a cup of tea, we caught up on our adult children who had known each other as teenagers. We shared stories of grandchildren and church. At one point, Cathy asked how I spent my time.

"I walk each day with my neighbor," I said. "We try to walk three miles a day. She's great company, and the exercise is good for both of us. We stop midway, sit on a bench overlooking the lake, and comment on everything from politics to nutrition to grandchildren."

Cathy responded, "One foot in front of the other."

"I guess it is," I answered.

I hadn't thought of it that way at the time, but my walking was a picture of my life in the past three plus years. It was about putting one foot in front of the other, taking a break as needed, and covering aspects of life that needed my attention.

German philosopher Friedrich Nietzsche said, "That which does not kill us makes us stronger." I have found that to be true. Each time I put one foot in front of the other to tackle an issue, I'm gaining strength. Every rest stop fills me for the next step.

In widowhood a dream is shattered; loss is real. At the same time, we grow and find positive things about ourselves we never knew. (My daughter Heather tells me I'm adding skills to my resume.) We can identify with other widows. We learn to ignore thoughtless comments and show grace. We refrain from giving platitudes to widows and others in areas we haven't experienced, such as loss of employment, financial reversals, or prodigal sons or daughters.

We've experienced losses and growth in our widowhood, but this we know: God accompanies us every step of the way. It's one foot in front of the other to move forward in His plans for us.

Treasured Reflections: What has putting one foot in front of the other meant to you? Progress? Gratitude? Uncertainty? Pain? Seeing God in new ways?

Treasured Thoughts: Journal your thoughts about your steps.

"My life is full of bounty, even as
I continue to feel the pain of loss.
Grace is transforming me, and it is
wonderful. I have slowly learned where
God belongs and have allowed him
to assume that place—at the center
of life rather than at the periphery."

Jerry Sittser, *A Grace Disguised*

57

A Tree Teaches a Lesson

I am the light of the world. Whoever follows me will
never walk in darkness, but will have the light of life.

JOHN 8:12

Since I planned to stay in town for Christmas, I decided to put up my Christmas tree. For the first time in years, I was genuinely looking forward to it. I headed to the attic, found the box, and attempted to pull out the tree. It wasn't as easy as I thought. The bulky tree comes in three heavy parts. I grabbed one piece, then reached into the box for another. I couldn't get hold of the third. If I tilted the box, I still had trouble getting a firm hold.

I stopped and contemplated the awkwardness of walking down attic steps carrying one heavy piece at a time, assembling the tree, and in January, disassembling and repacking. Reluctantly, I returned the pieces to the box and looked for another box marked "pencil tree." I opened containers of family ornaments and reminisced. They wouldn't work on a small tree. I admit I was disappointed.

Carrying the pencil tree from the attic to my living room was easy. I added a few strings of clear lights, several strings of dried berries, and fluffed a tree skirt to complete my project. Voila! In a matter of minutes, I had a tree; not quite what I had envisioned for spending Christmas in town, but it worked.

Later that evening, I lit the candles on my mantle and plugged in the tree lights. They sparkled. I sat on my couch and enjoyed the lights.

Although my expectations weren't met, I learned it wasn't about the tree or even the family decorations. Christmas is the season of light, celebrating Jesus, the Light of the world. He never leaves us and gives light in the darkness. I was content.

Treasured Reflections: On a scale of one to ten, where are you in anticipation of Christmas? There is no timetable for grief, but if you are past the "firsts" since your husband's passing, do you see your joy beginning to return?

Treasured Thoughts: Reflect on the changes in your outlook toward holidays since your husband died. What are your emotions at this point? Do you sense joy? How does Jesus comfort you and give you peace?

58

Holiday Gifts

Therefore encourage one another and build
one another up, just as you are doing.

1 THESSALONIANS 5:11 ESV

As I flipped through TV channels, a program on Christmas gift-wrapping caught my eye. I watched, amazed, as a woman turned an ordinary box into an elegant package. In just a few minutes, she wrapped the box with tissue paper and covered it with sparkling tulle in a complementary color. A wide satin wire ribbon embellished the package with an impressive bow. The box was breathtaking and could have been a table centerpiece.

Packages are not always elegant. Sometimes we receive packages containing something we wouldn't ask for or want. In December 2011, I was given a rough gift box—my husband's unexpected death two days before Christmas. I had no choice but to receive the box and open it.

Over the course of four years, I discovered the box held other contents besides loss. I sorted through layers of tissue. One layer held challenges. Another contained new experiences and a new status as a widow. I moved through layers of changes and decisions. The layers often held tears, loneliness, and sadness.

There were holidays in that box too. That deep layer had a confusing assortment. Like decorations individually wrapped in tissue, I unwrapped each holiday experience. Initially it felt like touching broken glass ornaments. I moved through questions: Do I put up and decorate a tree? How do I assemble the tree by myself? Should I travel to see one of my children or stay home? How do I manage joy with grandchildren when my heart is broken? Can I face a crowded mall? Am I up to going to a Christmas party?

By definition, a holiday is a festive time. Grief is a time of sorrow. *Sorrow* and *festivity* don't belong in the same sentence, much less occupy a person's heart at the same time. How does one grieve when others are celebrating? How do you manage festivity around you when your eyes are full of tears and life has irrevocably changed?

My box of grief with its multiple layers of loss was out of place that Christmas and didn't look beautiful under my tree. It was not even remotely what I wanted. But God delivered that box to me with the handpicked contents of challenges, tears, and changes.

Loss was magnified when everyone was celebrating. But wrapped in layers of tissue were God's grace, love, and wisdom. I sometimes found joy as I rummaged through the contents. I also found the gifts of ministering friends.

My widowed friend Ann invited me to attend a gingerbread house display the second year of my loss. "It's an unemotional way to step into the season," she said. It was a wise choice. And a good lesson. As a widowed friend of another widow, perhaps now I am handpicked to help another walk through her holiday grief. How can I show love to another broken heart?

Treasured Reflections: Each widow handles holidays in different ways. Your friends and family won't know your needs and wishes unless you share with them. Think of how you can minister to another widow.

Treasured Thoughts: Write about your anticipation and expectations regarding Christmas. What will be different? What traditions will you keep? If you are reading this after your "firsts," journal your thoughts on how subsequent holidays have changed.

The Presence of a Friend

Holidays are one of the most difficult and painful stops on the grief path.

Do you know another widow making that painful stop? How can you walk with her during this conflicting time of holiday grief? Most people are quick to offer support for a "first" holiday, but subsequent ones may be just as difficult or more so. The reality of finality sets in. Holidays will always have one less gift under the tree. When spent with family, holidays are also a reminder that the loss is permanent.

As you think about holiday and other celebrations, think about another's loss and how to minister to her. Every widow's grief and loss are unique and become different as months and years pass. There is no "one size fits all" for widows or their experiences.

In his book *The Five Love Languages*, Gary Chapman discusses ways to communicate love. Originally written for marriages, the five languages have also been used with parent/child relationships, the workplace, and friendships. Chapman says we express and receive love in different ways: words of affirmation, touch, quality time, acts of service, and gifts. Everyone has a primary and secondary love language.

Gifts of love may be *presents*, but more often it's one's expression and *presence* that makes a difference. So, this is a time for you, a widow, to be transparent in what you need and how you receive gifts. It can also be a healing time when you reach out to another widow and link arms with her.

Consider your genuine expression based on your personality and talents and your friend's love language, and respect the limits, needs, and priorities she sets. What might this look like?

Acts of service: Taking the artificial tree down from my attic was awkward. Assembling it with its color-coded branches seemed overwhelming.

Doing it alone magnified my loss. Can you offer help with decorating, putting holiday lights on shrubs, or hanging a wreath? Gift wrapping, mailing packages, and picking up stamps at the post office might be other ways to alleviate another widow's stress. Calling to say you're heading to a particular store and asking if you can pick something up for her lightens a load. Giving her a ride to the airport and picking her up on return are a gift not only in avoiding a parking garage with her luggage but reducing costs. Ask your friend what you can do for her.

Time is a precious commodity. Though you may think there isn't enough time to get everything done, another widow may feel her days are often too long and quiet. Can you offer to spend time with her or invite her to your home? Visiting and adding life to her quiet home is a gift in itself. Offering to bake a batch of cookies or make candy together or simply enjoying coffee or lunch together is a sweet gift of quality time. If she is up to attending a concert or taking a drive to view Christmas lights, offer to have her join you and your family or arrange a group of women to go together. A widow friend and I have a coffee phone call every Christmas morning.

Touch is a love language people often overlook. Those who express and receive love through touch especially miss the tactile expressions of love. The absence of touch is painful. I thought about that when my niece gave me a gift of a foot massage and someone else gave me the gift of a pedicure.

Words of affirmation can fuel someone for days. A widow has no one at home to tell her she looks nice or congratulate her on an accomplishment. Genuine encouragement and compliments (not platitudes or flattery) can change a countenance in seconds. My widowed friends applaud and encourage each other. Those words are gifts to us. One of the comments I hear from widows is that no one mentions her husband's name. Sharing a remembrance, "I remember the time . . ." is a gift. "Like apples of gold in settings of silver, is a word spoken at the proper time" (Proverbs 25:11 NASB).

Gifts are the most obvious expression, especially at Christmas. Dear friends had me to dinner, and we exchanged simple gifts. Another took me to lunch. Be creative in your gift giving. Gifts do not have to be extravagant or expensive. Christmas morning can be lonely. Suggest she save the gift to open Christmas day. When in doubt about a widowed friend's love language, ask. Still unsure about a gift? Pray before you call, and ask the Spirit to guide you.

59

Nourish the Body . . . Strengthen the Heart

Pure and genuine religion in the sight of God the
Father means caring for orphans and widows in their
distress and refusing to let the world corrupt you.

JAMES 1:27 NLT

Following my husband's death, Kate lived with me for several
months until she married. We were good company for each other.
"Why should each of us live alone?" she asked.

She'd put her townhouse on the market in preparation to move
after she married. It made sense to have a somewhat perfect, ready-to-
move-in impression for buyers.

One evening, she went out to dinner with her mentor, Jen. Kate ate
some of her grilled chicken salad and pushed most of it around her plate.

"Is that all you're eating?" Jen asked.

"Well, I'm not that hungry," Kate answered.

Jen probed. "Are you and your mother eating?"

"Yes," Kate answered tentatively.

"What do you eat?" Jen continued out of curiosity.

Kate paused. "Whatever my mom's neighbor fixes."

Kate went on to explain that my neighbor Lanette frequently had us
to dinner or made pans of food for us to eat or freeze later.

After Kate married, Lanette continued her mission. I ate at her home
more than my own. On one occasion, on a rainy fall day, I stayed in
sweats all day. Around 4 p.m., Lanette texted, "Dinner at 6:00. ☺" I
responded that I'd pass as I wasn't dressed.

A text came back, "Jerry said, 'Get over here. I'll wear a blindfold.'" I laughed at the response, washed my face, and put on makeup. With umbrella in hand, I walked next door. As always, it was a sweet time. I ate and I watched about an hour of TV with them. As I prepared to leave, I thanked them once again for their company and the meal.

"We're glad you came," Lanette said.

Jerry added, "I hope we put a smile on your face."

That they did. In eating with friends rather than alone, they not only nourished my body but strengthened my heart.

Treasured Reflections: Think about your invitations to a meal. How have those times refreshed you? Do you know of another widow who may be eating alone and could use your company?

Treasured Thoughts: Journal your thoughts about the nourishment you've received from others.

"The people who give you their food give you their heart."

Cesar Chavez, *An Organizer's Tale*

60

White Sand and Palm Trees

For the LORD is good and his love endures forever; his
faithfulness continues through all generations.

PSALM 100:5

My friend Ellen purchased a vacation membership that she and her family use several times a year. One winter she invited me to join her. She had accumulated thousands of "points" and free weeks. The invitation was hard to pass up. I drove to her home in Atlanta and then we flew to Cancun together, where we enjoyed a relaxing week and delicious food.

Due to decreased mobility, walking on the beach was not an option for Ellen, but she encouraged me to go and enjoy it. As I walked the white sand and basked in the beauty of the palm trees and crystal-like ocean, my mind went back to early married life.

Randy and I were married on a Saturday and flew to St. Thomas in the Virgin Islands the following Monday to begin teaching. For two plus years, we enjoyed paradise. Yes, we had the challenges of a high cost of living, adjusting to a different culture, and missing family for holidays, but it was an adventure of a lifetime and a great way to begin married life.

As I stood on the beach looking out at the ocean, my heart was stirred. It was a grace moment. Just as God had been with me in my past, allowing challenges, new experiences, and beauty, He was with me in my present and would be in my future. His faithfulness is never ending.

Treasured Reflections: Would going back to a significant place in your past (mentally, if not physically) stir your heart to remember God's provision and faithfulness? Just as there was good then, there will be good in your future.

Treasured Thoughts: Psalm 136 is a great psalm to read as you begin to journal thoughts about God's love, provision, and faithfulness.

"You do not heal from the death of a loved one because time passes; you heal because of what you do with the time."

Carol Staudacher, *A Time to Grieve*

61

Tears

You keep track of all my sorrows. You have collected all my
tears in your bottle.
You have recorded each one in your book.

PSALM 56:8 NLT

I met Judy in a corridor at church on Sunday morning and gave her
a hug. She'd been widowed three months earlier. We were talking
about how she was doing and the mounds of paperwork she was sort-
ing through, when a friend interrupted our conversation.

"I'm praying for you," she told Judy.

"Thank you, I need the prayer," Judy responded as her eyes filled
with tears.

"Oh, don't cry. Let's not have tears," her friend said as she patted
Judy's shoulder.

I'm not sure if I kept a straight face or looked appalled, but I wanted
to cheer for Judy as she answered, "No, I *need* to cry."

The woman just patted Judy and said, "Well, I'm praying for you."

The condescending gesture and tone sent chills up my arms.

I turned to Judy and gave her a grace moment: "Cry all you need to."

I appreciated Judy's boldness to set the record straight. Tears of grief
and sorrow are normal. They are necessary. Jesus wept at the news of
His friend Lazarus's death, and He is referred to in Scripture as a "Man
of sorrows and acquainted with grief" (Isaiah 53:3 NKJV).

Did you know that tears have a different composition depending
on their cause? Research has shown there is a difference between tears
of sorrow and the tears we shed when we peel an onion. Tears of
sorrow contain healing chemicals. Tears are God's provision. He has

wired us to cry. He considers tears so valuable that He records and stores each one.

"Don't cry." Are you serious? I hope not.

Treasured Reflections: Shedding tears is normal, healing, and designed by God. Tears are frequent in the early stages of grief and, fortunately, become less as time goes on. Thank Him for His gracious provision of tears and His timing in the lessening of our tears.

Treasured Thoughts: Journal thoughts about your tears, knowing God has stored them. Google the words "tears in grief" to learn more about their healing provision.

62

A New Resume

Do not despise these small beginnings, for the
LORD rejoices to see the work begin.

ZECHARIAH 4:10 NLT

One of the qualifications on my widowhood resume is marked "Acquisition of New Skills." Another is "New Adventures," and a third bears the heading, "Reluctant Independence." I have taken all three of those paths and have the credentials to include them on my resume.

Early in my widowhood, I faced the confusing task of organizing materials for taxes. Now I do it easily. Gardening was a pastime for my husband in retirement. Though I chose many of the flowering plants and shrubs, he planted and cared for them. Now if I want colorful flowers, I go to the nursery, read the labels, and opt for container gardening. I claim the prize for lifting, carrying via wheelbarrow, and laying 135 bags of mulch in my yard.

Probably my biggest accomplishment (aside from packing and moving to another state) was driving from North Carolina to my friend's house in Atlanta and then flying to Mexico with her. At the end of a week, Ellen stayed in Cancun, and I returned alone. I remember sitting in an airport alone waiting for my flight. I don't speak a word of Spanish. I wondered what my protective husband would think. He always cheered me on by saying, "You can do this," but this time, I imagine him shaking his head in disbelief.

In his poem *The Road Not Taken*, Robert Frost writes:

Two roads diverged in some wood, and I—
I took the one less traveled by,
And that has made all the difference.

Each statement in my widowhood resume was the result of a choice between fear or determination; being isolated or moving forward; picking myself up or hiding my head under the covers. I can't say I did all without tears, reluctance, or frustration. My best friend was absent. But each time, God gave me the strength and desire to move forward. That treasure has made all the difference in my growth.

Treasured Reflections: What are the qualifications and new skills on your resume that show growth since you became a widow? What helped you to move forward to do the next thing?

Treasured Thoughts: Journal your thoughts about your new resume. What surprises you?

"You may discover a whole range of new talent, but unless you take the first steps, your gifts may go unnoticed."

Eva Shaw, *What to Do When a Loved One Dies*

63

Love and a Soft Landing

A new command I give you: Love one another. As I
have loved you, so you must love one another.

JOHN 13:34

"You've really had a soft landing here, haven't you?" my friend
Louise said as we drove back from a prayer retreat.

"I never quite thought of it in those terms, but yes, a soft landing.
My relocations have not always been smooth. I've moved before and
cried for months in loneliness. Another move involved a major financial adjustment and stress. Moving here alone was difficult, but yes, I
suppose I'd agree with you." My neighbors welcomed me. I'm near
my family, have made sweet friends, and found my niche and ministry
at church.

My daughter's in-laws (who I prefer to call my friends and family
too), helped in my house-hunting when it was time for me to move.
Pam and Jeff knew the area well and could speak of advantages and
disadvantages of houses and neighborhoods. With experience behind
them, they computed the costs of home renovations and referred me to
businesses to contact when I considered options. If I enumerated ways
they helped me practically and with information from move-in day to
the present, the list would number in the triple digits.

We share grandchildren, celebrate holidays, and frequently eat Sunday lunch together. Jeff laughs because Pam and I are so similar that
we often show up at events wearing the same colors. If she calls, it's
when I'm just about to text her. I couldn't have planned a better or
more loving scenario.

I am humbled by their care for me, and at times I've resisted. It seems (and *is*) so one-sided. They are quick to point to James 1:27 as their willing commitment. Besides, "we like each other," Pam says.

One of the other aspects of my soft-landing move was finding other widows. Back in Charlotte, I was the only widow in my church and, aside from my friend Ann, knew no others. Given the size and age of the church I attend now, there are several. We get together for lunch the first Sunday of the month. I've hosted these friends for a Christmas brunch and a Valentine's Day lunch. For some it was their first Valentine's Day without their husband. I'm thankful my soft landing included meeting these women and ministering to them as they do to me. At lunch last week, one said I encouraged her. Puzzled, I responded, "How's that?"

"I lost my husband seven months ago. You show me there's hope and we can get through this."

"Days are not always easy," I said. "God knew what I needed when I needed it. His soft landing for me here was definitely part of His provision and grace. Loss is constant and permanent, but we can move forward."

Driving home from lunch that day, I thought about the conversation and was glad I could offer hope. I'm moving forward and at the point where I can comfort others. I miss being a wife. But I have come to realize marriage was a role, as is widowhood. Both are assignments from God, and neither is my identity. I am a daughter of the King, a child of God. My identity is in who I am in Christ. That is a treasure I have 24/7 for eternity.

Treasured Reflections: Are you at the place in your mourning labyrinth where you can offer comfort and the benefit of experience to other widows? More than anything else, do you know the grace of being God's child?

Treasured Thoughts: Journal thoughts about landing in a new place—whether through moving or through finding a new group of friends and new opportunities—confident that God accompanies and loves you.

"You can't go back and make a new
start, but you can start right now
and make a brand-new ending."

James R. Sherman, *Rejection*

64

Treasures in
White Powdered Donuts

Praise the LORD. Give thanks to the LORD, for
he is good; his love endures forever.

PSALM 106:1

Last week I had the gift of spending five days at the beach with
friends. What would have been my forty-eighth wedding anniversary took place in the middle of the week. That morning I grabbed a
cup of coffee, my Bible, and several small, white powdered doughnuts
and walked to the beach alone.

I told my friends—all widows—that whenever our family took beach
vacations, at least one breakfast was marked with powdered doughnuts
on the beach. It was a sweet tradition observed early in the morning
and on a quiet beach. So, tradition told me since I was at the beach, I
would mark my anniversary, albeit alone, with the same.

I sat looking at the magnificence of the ocean, waves coming in with
regularity, a gorgeous blue sky dotted with white clouds—God's gran-
deur in full view. I remembered my seasons of God-given joy: children
building sandcastles, my husband fishing, grandchildren splashing, past
anniversaries . . .

And I opened my Bible to Psalm 106:1: "Praise the LORD. Give
thanks to the LORD, for he is good; his love endures forever."

I marked the date in my Bible. On my sixth anniversary without
my husband, the beach is still my beautiful peaceful place. The waves
come and recede, so similar to the changing sting of grief and loss, and

the sun still shines. Treasures of truth remain: God is always good, and His love lasts forever. I rest in those markers and give thanks.

Treasured Reflections: What markers do you have that remind you of God's care? Have you kept any rituals or traditions to mark your anniversary or your husband's birthday?

Treasured Thoughts: Read Psalm 106 and journal your thoughts.

"Say not in grief 'he is no more'
but in thankfulness that he was."

Hebrew proverb

65

A Painful Visual Aid

He makes my feet like the feet of a deer; he
causes me to stand on the heights.

PSALM 18:33

When I lived in Charlotte, I walked six or seven days a week. My neighbor and I had a regular schedule, and we clocked nearly three miles each time. It was also therapeutic. It gave us company as we walked and it had relational, mental, and physical benefits.

At one point, I developed leg pain that interrupted my walking. When I moved to South Carolina, I was engrossed in getting settled and put walking on the back burner. Once I started walking regularly again, I could hardly go a half mile. I prayed for relief. I tried over-the-counter painkillers. When I could barely walk a quarter mile, I sought medical advice. I had X-rays, tried acupuncture, and then began physical therapy. I saw gradual improvement.

Yesterday I walked the track at my church's recreation center. I thought about my leg pain, and now the absence of it, as I made another lap. I'm up to three miles again pain-free. It's been gradual, but I'm making progress.

I had an aha moment—a treasure—as I thanked God that I could once again walk a distance. It was a picture of my grief journey: pain, coming to a stop, incremental progress, and now going longer distances with more confidence, resolution, and joy. God has been my accompaniment in each place—for both my leg pain and the pain in my heart.

Treasured Reflections: Have you had an aha moment where the progress in your grief and mourning is apparent?

Treasured Thoughts: Journal your thoughts about your healing and the promise that God desires to heal the brokenhearted. (Read Psalm 147:3.)

Physical Responses to Grief

I never had serious health issues until two months after my husband died. The intermittent shooting pain in my right leg couldn't be ignored. I sought medical help. The diagnosis was a sciatica-like condition, and physical therapy was prescribed. During a conversation with my physical therapist, I mentioned my former good health. Was it age? Some sort of trauma to my leg I was unaware of? He casually mentioned that traumatic events can bring on physical problems. Interesting. Yes, I had had a traumatic event, and I was still living in it.

A few years later, as a facilitator for a grief support group, I picked up *The Grieving Journey*. This concise booklet gave helpful practical information but also a list of physical responses to grief:

- Recurring headaches
- Lung issues such as bronchitis, viral infections, coughs, pneumonia
- Muscle or joint aches, throwing out your back, sciatica
- Sensitivity to loud noises
- Depressed immune response
- Pains or ailments in the same location as the ailment/injury of the deceased
- Rashes or outbreaks on the skin

We're sad and have new decisions to make, and health issues compound our challenges. Recognizing these physical responses to grief and loss is helpful as you begin to heal. If you are experiencing physical changes, seek medical attention to determine your next steps.

"The sorrow which has no vent in tears may make other organs weep."

Henry Maudsley, *The Pathology of Mind*

EPILOGUE
Endless Grace

Praise be to the God and Father of our Lord Jesus Christ, the
Father of compassion and the God of all comfort, who comforts
us in all our troubles, so that we can comfort those in any
trouble with the comfort we ourselves receive from God.

2 CORINTHIANS 1:3–4

Someone asked me why I chose the number of reflections found
here. I answered candidly, "I had to stop somewhere. This is an
endless journey."

So, sixty-five entries later, I wrote my final thought for this book.
But we know there's not a final scene in a journey accompanied by
loss, nor do we stop finding treasures in life. My personal journal entries continue, as I hope yours will too.

Recently, while shopping with a friend, we read a plaque that said,
"Grief doesn't know an expiration date." Living with loss looks different as time progresses. We find a new perspective, new strength,
and new opportunities, sometimes finding ourselves in surprising new
adventures. We begin to move outside of ourselves and extend comfort
and advice to those beginning their grief journey. Ongoing evidence
of God's faithfulness and grace enriches others with hope; and at the
right time, we help others find their treasures.

When I attended my youngest grandson's school chapel last year,
my eyes filled with tears as he and the other children sang about how

all good gifts come from God. Enumerating each gift from family to the air we breathe, the children sang with gratitude for daily blessings. My mind went back to the last time Randy and I attended our oldest grands' chapel. They were five and seven at the time, and we had no idea Randy would be gone in mere days. A few years later, I attended again—alone—and sang along with them about God's amazing grace. It is amazing and endless with countless opportunities for gratitude. God's gifts have shown up in every passage and page of my life and will continue, just as they will for you. The treasures are there. Don't miss them.

Treasured Reflections: Our future has blank pages ready to be filled. My prayer is that you will be aware of, and record, the treasures, with joy and gratitude for God's faithfulness. Every day there's something to be thankful for and appreciate about your life. Add to the list each day or weekly. You will begin to see positive aspects of your life, even though your life is much different. God desires we live meaningful and purposeful lives and offers us amazing and endless grace to do it. He will not waste our pain. May we comfort others with the comfort we have been given, and honor God by leaning into life, living with His purposes.

Treasured Thoughts: Journal your thoughts about the words from my cruise, "Don't compare, and don't miss the treasures."

Blessings to you, as you move forward in His grace and continue to look in order to see.

—Marilyn

"You will lose someone you can't live without, and your heart will be badly broken, and the bad news is that you never completely get over the loss of your beloved. But this is also the good news. They live forever in your broken heart that doesn't seal back up. And you come through. It's like having a broken leg that never heals perfectly—that still hurts when the weather gets cold, but you learn to dance with the limp."

Anne Lamott, *Plan B*

Your White Space
What will you write in your life and in your journal?

You gain strength, courage and confidence by every experience in which you really stop to look fear in the face. You are able to say to yourself, "I have lived through this horror. I can take the next thing that comes along." You must do the thing you think you cannot do.

        —Eleanor Roosevelt, *You Learn by Living*

Goals, opportunities, friendships, plans, spiritual gifts, talents, dreams, skills, new hobby, ministries, family, grandchildren, reading, . . .

POSTSCRIPT

Eleven Years Later
Leaning into Life

I scanned the greeting card rack looking for a "Thinking of You" card to send to a friend. The selection covered a spectrum of formal notes, humorous drawings, and syrupy rhymes. A few cards were misplaced, probably by busy shoppers. One caught my eye, "In Appreciation." Not what I was looking for, but the phrase held my attention.

In appreciation of . . .

Eleven years have passed since I heard unexpected words that altered my life. In those 4,000 plus days, I've run the gamut of emotions and thoughts, experienced challenges and successes, met new people, traveled to new places—and I still miss my husband.

I have also learned and developed appreciation. Loss is as unique as a snowflake, and my appreciation list may not be yours, but I encourage you to look for hope and gratitude as you make a list and reflect on your new widowhood journey.

When I lived in Charlotte, I had many friends, but I was the only widow in my church. When I relocated to another state to be near family, I met four widows who became my friends. Let me clarify—best friends. Last Sunday, I hosted our widows' Sunday lunch bunch at my house and nineteen attended. On Friday night, fourteen were at our Bible study. These are the women I "do life" with. "Doing life" is what we're doing. In our doing, we're encouraging, growing, and becoming. We share real circumstances and disappointments with no judgment. I appreciate them. Some have been widowed longer than I, some much less. We appreciate the opportunity to see 2 Corinthians 1:3–4 come alive: "Praise be to the God and Father of our Lord Jesus Christ, the Father of compassion and the God of all comfort, who comforts us in all our troubles, so that we can comfort those in any trouble with the comfort we ourselves receive from God." As months moved forward into years, life happened, and my family has grown. Randy was present in the delivery room when our first grandchild entered the world. Last year, that sweet girl graduated from high school and is now a college student. Seeing her walk across the stage at commencement took me back to milestones in her life, all we shared as a "Nonni and Papa" for seven years. I put my wedding ring back on for that day and my daughter wore pearl earrings her dad had given her.

The grands' personalities and interests are all different, and I appreciate their uniqueness and contribution to our family. I also appreciate the coordination of dates my daughters work toward so all fifteen of us can gather around my table for our annual summer reunion. Randy knew four grands under seven. Six of the eight grands are teenagers, more evidence of how time has passed. It's pure delight to be together, but we still notice the empty chair.

My move to South Carolina led me to a church where I could administer and facilitate a grief support group for spouses. A grief program that limits its ministry to the loss of a spouse is unique, and I am thankful to be part of it and come alongside other grievers and guide them toward healing.

I appreciate knowing the difference between moving forward and moving on. Sixteen-year-old girls who break up with boyfriends move on. Widows do not move on to the next thing or person but move forward in their assignment. Yes, I have learned to appreciate widowhood as an assignment. Just as being a wife was a role and assignment, so is widowhood. It's a hard one with steps of unfamiliarity and uncertainty often woven with loneliness and a status we didn't seek or want. Yet, as Ephesians 2:10 says, God has prepared works in advance for us to do. I remember the words of Psalm 16:5: "Lord, . . . you make my lot secure."

When I reflect on what I've learned and experienced in eleven years, I'm overcome by incredulity that I've lived a solo life—never on my radar at my age. Yet I marvel at God's faithfulness: providing people for encouragement, recreation, and help when I needed it; ideas for writing; consolation, strength, and grace; opportunities in ministry. Incredulity led to overwhelming and then overflowing appreciation for God's provisions.

I began *Hope for Widows* by sharing about our anniversary cruise to Alaska. Last summer I took a solo road trip covering 2,393 miles (you read that right) to see friends and family I hadn't seen in years due to COVID-19 and life interruptions. I was thankful for a GPS and audio because looking down at a map on an interstate is not smart! I stopped at places where my husband and I lived and worked, had lunch with women who were part of a Bible study forty-five years ago, visited with my college roommate and friends, and reminisced with family about our upbringing. I didn't shop or sightsee except for visiting places associated with memories—having an ice-cream cone at the lake and shopping at a favorite supermarket—but spent days in conversation and long walks. I didn't watch TV during the entire trip and opened my laptop briefly twice out of necessity.

When I pulled into my driveway thirteen days later, I sighed with relief, thanks, and amazement for the roads I traveled and where they took me. Just as in Alaska, I had experiences money couldn't buy and saw sights not made by man. So, I end with the same encouragement I started with: *Don't miss the treasures* in the moment. Value personal growth, people, experiences, and the grace God gives. Grow in gratitude, live in appreciation, and look for treasures, even now, in a new assignment.

God from A to Z

I am the Alpha and the Omega, the First and
the Last, the Beginning and the End.

REVELATION 22:13

One of the exercises I did in a Bible study years ago was to reflect on
the character of God. Our group listed qualities using letters of the
alphabet from A to Z. It's encouraging to know God is each of these
characteristics and every one of them is available to us. You may want
to write what you know about God from A to Z and later find the
Bible verses that remind you of that truth. Trust me, you will be comforted. To get you started:

A: all-powerful, all-knowing, all-seeing, amazing

B: beautiful, bountiful

C: creator, caring

Prayers

In the New Testament, the apostle Paul wrote letters to churches that included prayers. His prayers were not for tangible items, but for knowing God in deeper ways. As we travel our grief and mourning journey, our greatest gift to ourselves is developing a closer walk with God. Fill your name in the verses below as an offering to God, asking Him to work in you.

God delights in answering "yes."

I keep asking that the God of our Lord Jesus Christ, the glorious Father, may give you the Spirit of wisdom and revelation, so that you may know him better. I pray that the eyes of your heart may be enlightened in order that you may know the hope to which he has called you, the riches of his glorious inheritance in his holy people, and his incomparably great power for us who believe. That power is the same as the mighty strength he exerted when he raised Christ from the dead and seated him at his right hand in the heavenly realms, far above all rule and authority, power and dominion, and every name that is invoked, not only in the present age but also in the one to come. (Ephesians 1:17–21)

For this reason I kneel before the Father, from whom every family in heaven and on earth derives its name. I pray that out of his glorious riches he may strengthen you with power through his Spirit in your inner being, so that Christ may dwell in your hearts through faith. And I pray that you, being rooted and established in love, may have power, together with all the Lord's holy people, to grasp how wide and long and high and deep is the love of Christ, and to know this love that surpasses knowledge—that you may be filled to the measure of all the fullness of God.

Now to him who is able to do immeasurably more than all we ask or imagine, according to his power that is at work within us, to him be glory in the church and in Christ Jesus throughout all generations, for ever and ever! Amen. (Ephesians 3:14–21)

I always pray with joy because of your partnership in the gospel from the first day until now, being confident of this, that he who began a good work in you will carry it on to completion until the day of Christ Jesus. (Philippians 1:4–6)

We continually ask God to fill you with the knowledge of his will through all the wisdom and understanding that the Spirit gives, so that you may live a life worthy of the Lord and please him in every way: bearing fruit in every good work, growing in the knowledge of God, being strengthened with all power according to his glorious might so that you may have great endurance and patience, and giving joyful thanks to the Father, who has qualified you to share in the inheritance of his holy people in the kingdom of light. For he has rescued us from the dominion of darkness and brought us into the kingdom of the Son he loves, in whom we have redemption, the forgiveness of sins. (Colossians 1:9–14)

ACKNOWLEDGMENTS

I want to acknowledge many who have been behind the scenes to see *Hope for Widows* come to the printed page. Thank you to:

Janet Grant, president and founder of Books & Such Literary Management, and Rachel Kent, my agent, who saw the need and vision to give widows a voice. Your words and affirmation of its value encouraged me more than you know.

Dawn Anderson and the staff of Our Daily Bread Publishing, for accepting *Hope for Widows*, seeing the reality of grief, and offering a way for women to see life ahead, even in dramatic change.

Alyson Kieda for your insightful and clear editing.

Fellow writers who offered critiques, support, and prayers for years: April, Jeannie, Katy, and Tammy, among many others in critique groups.

Lori Hatcher, who read a version of the manuscript years ago and motivated me to keep going.

Louise, my first friend when I moved to Greer, who invited me to live and play, showing we have promise ahead of us.

Dot, Peggy, and Rosemary, new God-given friends, for opportunities of laughter and honest conversations, the joy of finding surprising God-moments together, and their interest and prayers as they tried to understand the writing journey.

Local and faraway friends and family who raised my spirits through conversations, texts, and prayers.

My friends in Charlotte who, in their shock, walked with me in my greatest life change.

Pam and Jeff for taking James 1:27 seriously when I relocated and inviting me into their family.

My daughters and their husbands—Heather and Paul, Susan and Jon, Kate and Doug—and my grandchildren, who bring love to me every time we meet and show me answers Dad and I prayed for.

My Lord and Savior Jesus, whose daily mercies, compassions, and faithfulness never cease and get me through every day. Thank you for the gift of writing for you. May it bring you honor.

Spread the Word
by Doing One Thing.

- Give a copy of this book as a gift.
- Share the QR code link via your social media.
- Write a review of this book on your blog, favorite bookseller's website, or at ODB.org/store.
- Recommend this book to your church, small group, or book club.

❀ Our Daily Bread

Connect with us. 🅕 ◎ 𝕐

Our Daily Bread Publishing
PO Box 3566, Grand Rapids, MI 49501, USA
Email: books@odb.org

Love God. Love Others.

with  Our Daily Bread.

Your gift changes lives.

Connect with us.

Our Daily Bread Publishing
PO Box 3566, Grand Rapids, MI 49501, USA
Email: books@odb.org